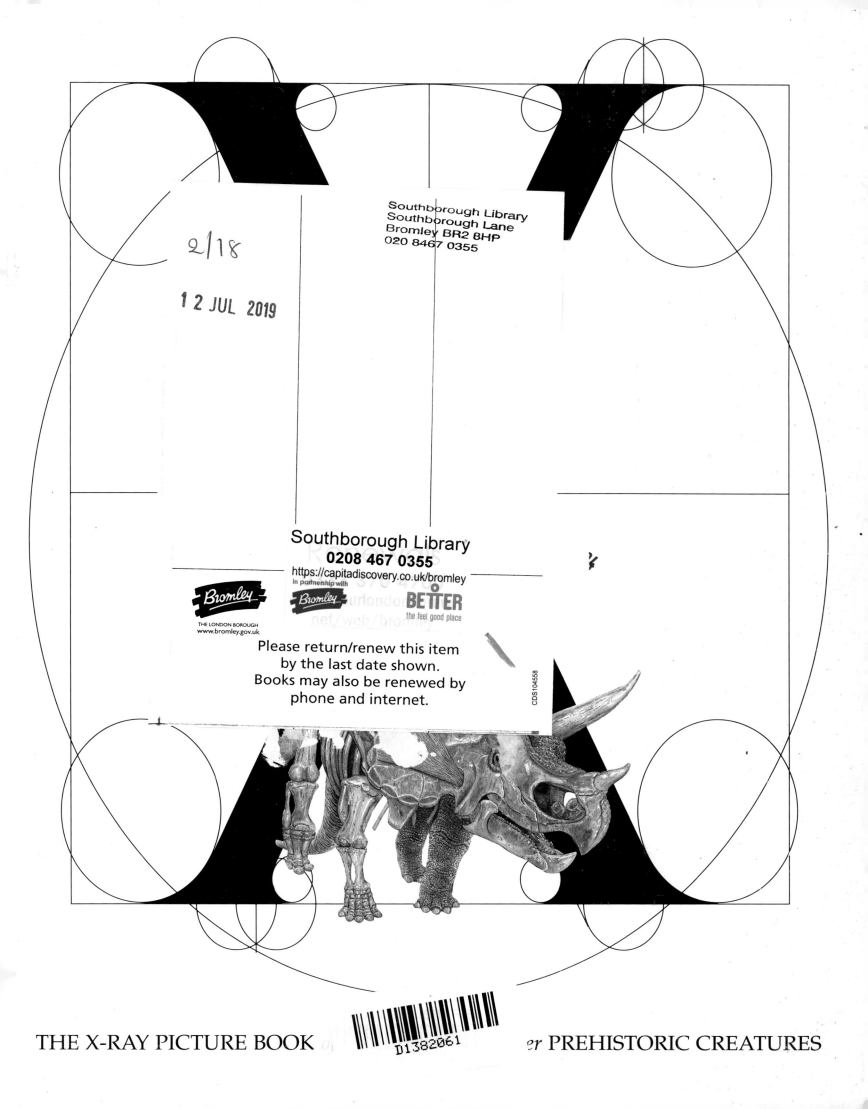

2/18

1 2 JUL 2019

THE X-RAY PICTURE BOOK of PREHISTORIC CREATURES

Author:

Dr Kathryn Senior is a former biomedical research scientist who studied at Cambridge University for a first degree in Pathology and a doctorate in Microbiology. After four years in research she joined the world of publishing, working as an editor of children's science books. She has also written *Timelines:Medicine* and *The X-ray Picture Book of Your Body* for Watts. Dr Senior is now a freelance writer and editor living in Berkshire.

Creator:

David Salariya was born in Dundee, Scotland, where he studied illustration and printmaking, concentrating on book design in his post-graduate year. He has illustrated a wide range of books on botanical, historical and mythical subjects. He has designed and created the *Timelines*, *New View* and *X-ray Picture Book* series for Watts. He lives in Brighton with his wife, the illustrator Shirley Willis.

Consultant:

John A. Cooper is Keeper of Geology and Keeper of the Booth Museum of Natural History in Brighton. He has previously worked in Leicestershire Museums and has held a 6-month fellowship at the Carnegie Museum of Natural History in Pittsburgh, USA, where he studied dinosaurs. He has written two books on dinosaurs and has been consultant on many others. He has a degree in Geology and a Postgraduate Diploma in Museum Studies from Leicester University.

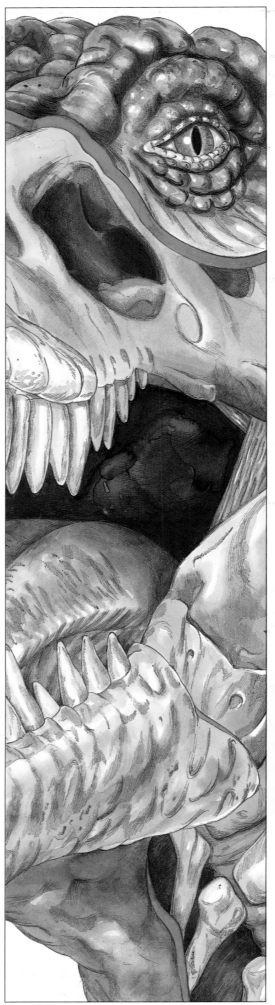

First Published in 1994
by Franklin Watts
This edition 2001

Franklin Watts
96 Leonard Street, London EC2A 4XD

Franklin Watts Australia
56 O'Riordan Street
Alexandria, Sydney, NSW 2015

ISBN 0 7496 4141 X

David Salariya	*Series Editor*
Ruth Nason	*Senior Editor*
Penny Clarke	*Book Editor*
John A. Cooper	*Consultant*

Artist

Carolyn Scrace is a graduate of Brighton College of Art who specialized in illustration. She illustrated her first book while still at school. She has worked in animation, advertising and children's non-fiction and enjoys natural history illustration. She is a major contributor to the *X-Ray Picture Book* series, in particular *Amazing Animals* and *Your Body*.

The X RAY
PICTURE BOOK of

DINOSAURS
& OTHER PREHISTORIC
CREATURES

Written by

KATHRYN SENIOR

Illustrated by

CAROLYN SCRACE

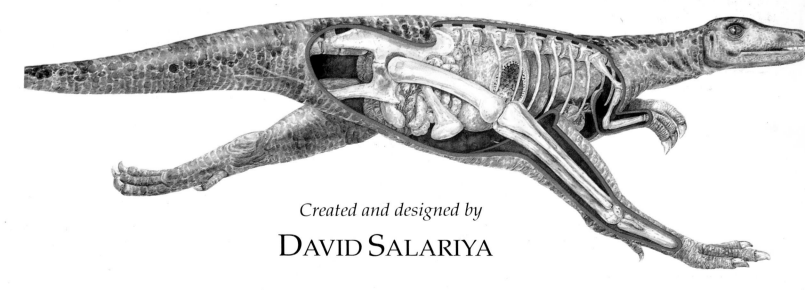

Created and designed by

DAVID SALARIYA

W
FRANKLIN WATTS
LONDON·SYDNEY

CONTENTS

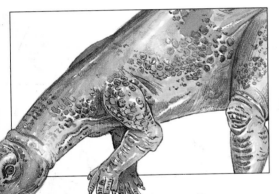

ARMOUR-PLATED DINOSAURS

DINOSAUR REPRODUCTION

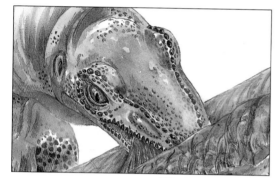

FIGHTING FOR SURVIVAL

OTHER PREHISTORIC ANIMALS

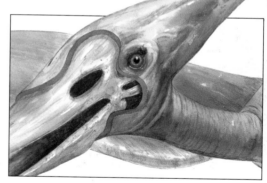

MYSTERIES AND MYTHS

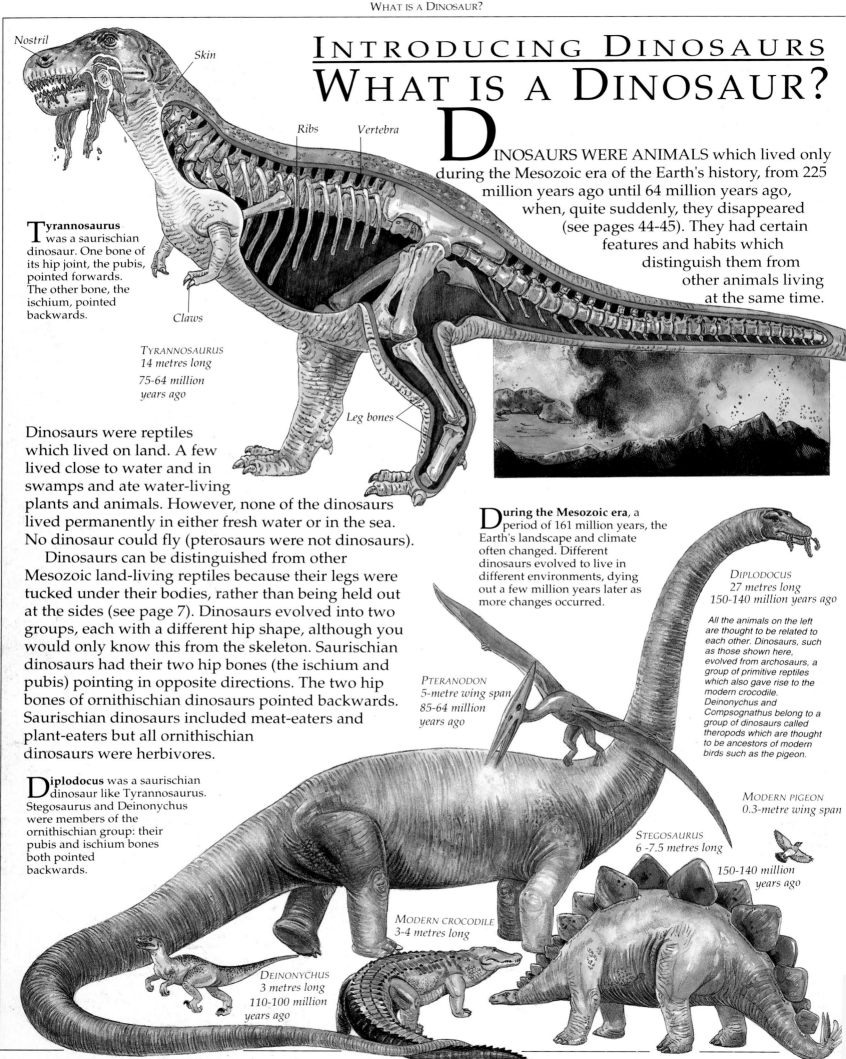

INTRODUCING DINOSAURS
WHAT IS A DINOSAUR?

Nostril

Skin

Ribs   *Vertebra*

Tyrannosaurus was a saurischian dinosaur. One bone of its hip joint, the pubis, pointed forwards. The other bone, the ischium, pointed backwards.

Claws

TYRANNOSAURUS
14 metres long
75-64 million years ago

Leg bones

DINOSAURS WERE ANIMALS which lived only during the Mesozoic era of the Earth's history, from 225 million years ago until 64 million years ago, when, quite suddenly, they disappeared (see pages 44-45). They had certain features and habits which distinguish them from other animals living at the same time.

Dinosaurs were reptiles which lived on land. A few lived close to water and in swamps and ate water-living plants and animals. However, none of the dinosaurs lived permanently in either fresh water or in the sea. No dinosaur could fly (pterosaurs were not dinosaurs).

Dinosaurs can be distinguished from other Mesozoic land-living reptiles because their legs were tucked under their bodies, rather than being held out at the sides (see page 7). Dinosaurs evolved into two groups, each with a different hip shape, although you would only know this from the skeleton. Saurischian dinosaurs had their two hip bones (the ischium and pubis) pointing in opposite directions. The two hip bones of ornithischian dinosaurs pointed backwards. Saurischian dinosaurs included meat-eaters and plant-eaters but all ornithischian dinosaurs were herbivores.

Diplodocus was a saurischian dinosaur like Tyrannosaurus. Stegosaurus and Deinonychus were members of the ornithischian group: their pubis and ischium bones both pointed backwards.

During the Mesozoic era, a period of 161 million years, the Earth's landscape and climate often changed. Different dinosaurs evolved to live in different environments, dying out a few million years later as more changes occurred.

DIPLODOCUS
27 metres long
150-140 million years ago

All the animals on the left are thought to be related to each other. Dinosaurs, such as those shown here, evolved from archosaurs, a group of primitive reptiles which also gave rise to the modern crocodile. Deinonychus and Compsognathus belong to a group of dinosaurs called theropods which are thought to be ancestors of modern birds such as the pigeon.

PTERANODON
5-metre wing span
85-64 million years ago

MODERN PIGEON
0.3-metre wing span

STEGOSAURUS
6 -7.5 metres long

150-140 million years ago

MODERN CROCODILE
3-4 metres long

DEINONYCHUS
3 metres long
110-100 million years ago

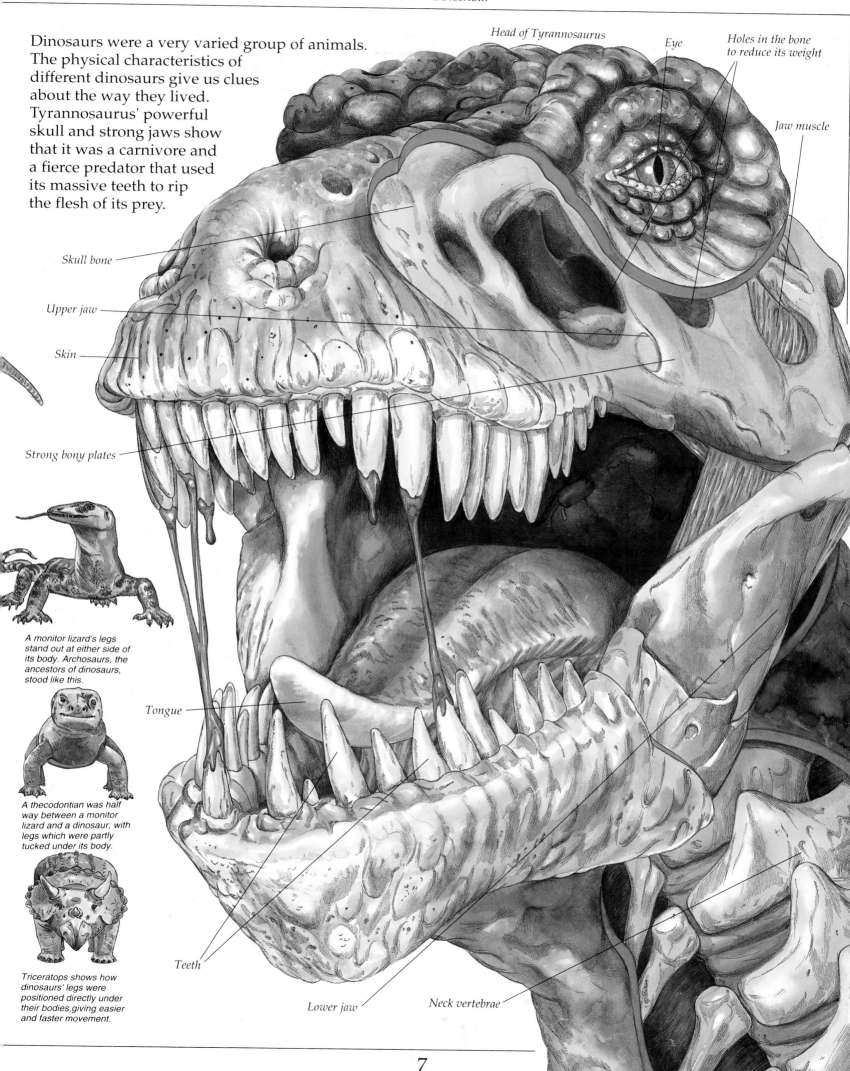

Dinosaurs were a very varied group of animals. The physical characteristics of different dinosaurs give us clues about the way they lived. Tyrannosaurus' powerful skull and strong jaws show that it was a carnivore and a fierce predator that used its massive teeth to rip the flesh of its prey.

Head of Tyrannosaurus

Eye

Holes in the bone to reduce its weight

Jaw muscle

Skull bone

Upper jaw

Skin

Strong bony plates

A monitor lizard's legs stand out at either side of its body. Archosaurs, the ancestors of dinosaurs, stood like this.

A thecodontian was half way between a monitor lizard and a dinosaur, with legs which were partly tucked under its body.

Tongue

Triceratops shows how dinosaurs' legs were positioned directly under their bodies, giving easier and faster movement.

Teeth

Lower jaw

Neck vertebrae

INTRODUCING DINOSAURS

THE AGE OF THE DINOSAURS

SCIENTISTS USUALLY SPLIT THE MESOZOIC ERA - the Age of the Dinosaurs - into three separate periods: the Triassic period (225-200 million years ago), the Jurassic period (200-135 million years ago) and the Cretaceous period (135-64 million years ago). Dinosaurs began to appear during the Triassic period and, by the end of that time, were the dominant form of animal life.

Many different types of dinosaur existed during the Mesozoic era. They were extremely varied, ranging in size from Compsognathus, which was only seventy centimetres long, to Brachiosaurus, the most massive dinosaur which ever lived. Brachiosaurus was an incredible twenty-seven metres long, and weighed over 80,000 kilograms. Some ate only plants, others were active hunters and ate other dinosaurs and some developed digestive systems which could cope with almost anything.

Throughout the Earth's early history the shapes of its land masses were very different from today. When dinosaurs existed many parts of the world which are now separated by thousands of miles of ocean were joined together. Over the millions of years which have passed since dinosaurs first evolved, the land masses have moved apart, giving today's widely spread continents. Reading from the bottom up, the six diagrams (left) show this evolution.

End of the Cretaceous period

Eudimorphodon

Rhamphorhynchus

Archaeopteryx

Start of the Cretaceous period

The Cretaceous period (135-64 million years ago). Modern fish, flowering plants and birds evolved. 64 million years ago there was a mass extinction and dinosaurs and many other living things died out.

The Jurassic period (200-135 million years ago). Dinosaurs were abundant on land, pterosaurs ruled the air and ichthyosaurs and plesiosaurs dominated the oceans. Archaeopteryx evolved.

The Triassic period (225-200 million years ago). The first dinosaurs evolved from primitive reptiles at the start of this period. True mammals began to appear towards the end of this period.

8

Start of the Jurassic period

⑩ ⑧ ⑥ ④

② ①

Start of the Triassic period

The time spiral above represents the Mesozoic era. The spiral starts at the bottom, showing the Earth 225 million years ago, at the beginning of the Triassic period (225-200 million years ago). It winds upwards, showing the Jurassic period (200-135 million years ago) and the Cretaceous period (135-64 million years ago). It stops at the end of the Cretaceous period, 64 million years ago, when the dinosaurs and many other prehistoric creatures became extinct. The positions of the dinosaur illustrations beside the spiral show when each of them lived (see caption at the bottom right of this page).

Dinosaur fossils have been found on every continent. It is unlikely that fossils of all the different types of dinosaur which existed have been found, but those that have been recovered tell us a lot. They show where on Earth certain types of dinosaur lived and when they died, and they give us clues about the habits of the dinosaurs. However, there are so few clear-cut facts about dinosaurs that many things about them are still hotly debated. The discovery of new fossils may help us to unravel some of the mysteries, such as the reason for the mass extinction of the dinosaurs and many other forms of life 64 million years ago (see pages 44-45).

The prehistoric animals on the time spiral are: 1 Coleophysis, 2 Staurikosaurus, 3 Lagosuchus, 4 Shonisaurus, 5 Plateosaurus, 6 Lesothosaurus, 7 Anchisaurus, 8 Heterodontosaurus, 9 Dilophosaurus, 10 Segisaurus, 11 Stegosaurus, 12 Diplodocus, 13 Iguanodon, 14 Elasmosaurus, 15 Psittacosaurus, 16 Protoceratops, 17 Pachycephalosaurus, 18 Parasaurolophus, 19 Triceratops and 20 Tyrannosaurus. Eudimorphodon, Rhamphorhynchus and Archaeopteryx are flying around in the middle of the spiral. (The creatures are not drawn to scale.)

⑨ ⑦ ⑤ ③

The Permian period (286-225 million years ago). The Earth was hit by long droughts and huge deserts formed. The reptiles continued to evolve, becoming mammal-like animals.

The Carboniferous period (360-286 million years ago). Amphibians continued to thrive and reptiles evolved. Primitive vascular plants formed forests which later fossilized to form coal deposits.

The Earth in the early Devonian period of history (408-360 million years ago). Land-living invertebrates existed and there were many vascular land plants. Amphibians evolved from air-breathing fish.

Dilophosaurus was the earliest large carnivorous dinosaur, living 190 to 180 million years ago. Its skull had a series of bony plates which formed a crest on the forehead. It was probably a scavenger, not an active hunter.

Crest

CARNIVOROUS DINOSAURS
THE KILLER GIANTS

TWO DISTINCT GROUPS of carnivorous theropod dinosaur evolved. (These were dinosaurs that walked on two feet.) The first group appeared between 190 and 150 million years ago, during the Jurassic period, and included Allosaurus, Ceratosaurus and Dilophosaurus. The second group, which dates from the very end of the Cretaceous period, between 75 and 64 million years ago, included Tyrannosaurus, Albertosaurus and Daspletosaurus (see page 11).

Both groups had large, powerful back legs with clawed feet. Their strong jaws contained huge, pointed teeth for tearing flesh. Their skulls were formed from thick bone to withstand the jarring when they clamped their jaws shut. The bones of the skull were not solid. They contained holes, which lightened the skull so that the head was not too heavy for the neck.

Allosaurus lived 150 to 125 million years ago. It was 12 metres long and stood about 3 metres off the ground.

Ceratosaurus lived at the same time as Allosaurus but was a smaller dinosaur. It was 6 metres long and 2 metres high.

ALLOSAURUS
12 metres long
150-125 million years ago

CERATOSAURUS
6 metres long
150-125 million years ago

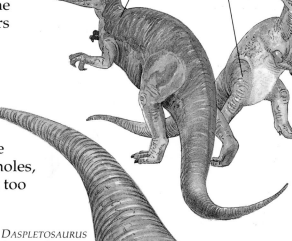

DILOPHOSAURUS
6 metres long
190-180 million years ago

GETTING UP

A resting tyrannosaur (top) probably lay on its stomach. Getting up may have proved difficult because of its weight.

Some dinosaur experts think that the small front legs balanced the animal as it started to rise.

When the back legs were almost straight the dinosaur would throw its head back, pulling it up from the ground.

After this great effort the tyrannosaur would be fully upright and ready to go off to search for food.

TYRANNOSAURUS
14 metres long
75-64 million years ago

ALBERTOSAURUS
9 metres long
75-64 million years ago

DASPLETOSAURUS
9 metres long
75-64 million years ago

Tyrannosaurus was the largest carnivorous dinosaur that ever lived. It was 14 metres long, 5 metres high and weighed over 7000 kg. It probably hunted alone but it may also have been a scavenger, taking advantage of large kills made by other dinosaurs.

Albertosaurus and Daspletosaurus were smaller relatives of Tyrannosaurus, measuring 9 metres from head to tail tip. Albertosaurus hunted hadrosaurs (see page 28) whilst Daspletosaurus hunted armoured ceratopids (see page 29).

Once a tyrannosaur had killed its prey it dismembered and ate it quickly: a rotting carcass would have attracted scavengers from miles around. The large dagger-like teeth would have been used to slice through the carcass. The strong neck muscles would have helped it to pull great chunks of flesh off the body, which it then swallowed whole.

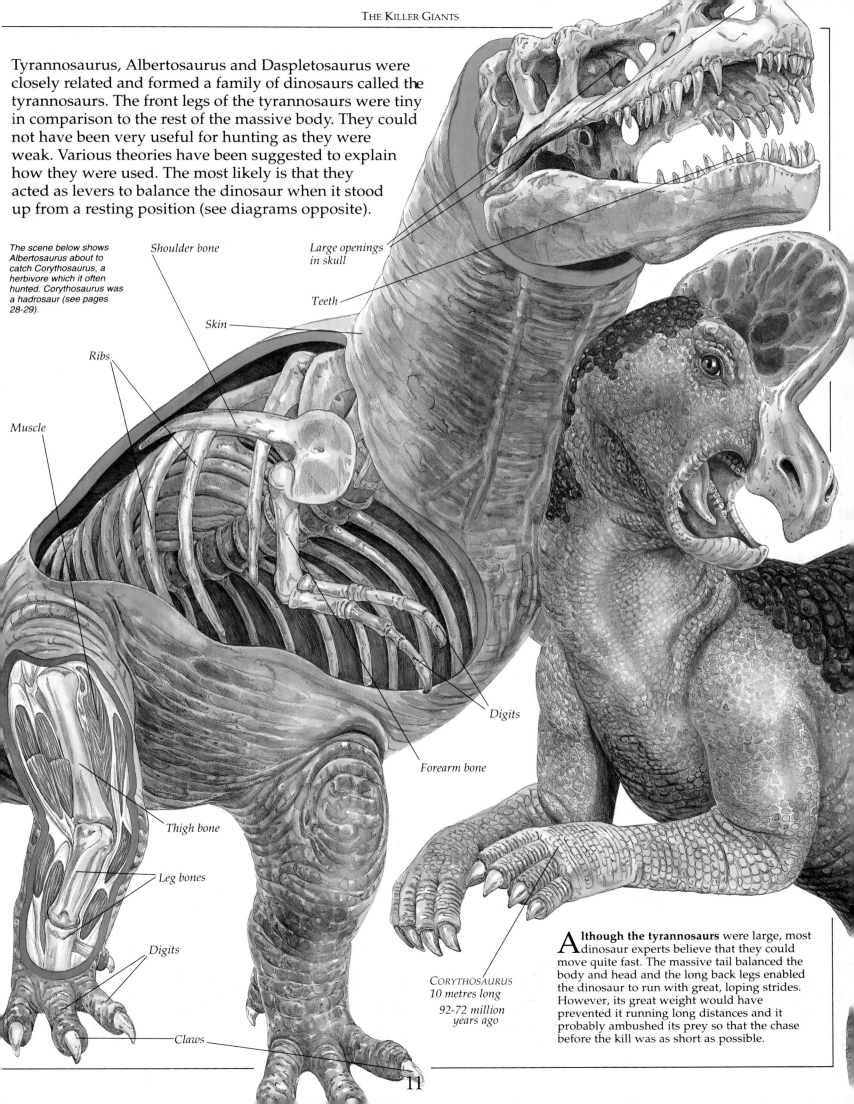

Tyrannosaurus, Albertosaurus and Daspletosaurus were closely related and formed a family of dinosaurs called the tyrannosaurs. The front legs of the tyrannosaurs were tiny in comparison to the rest of the massive body. They could not have been very useful for hunting as they were weak. Various theories have been suggested to explain how they were used. The most likely is that they acted as levers to balance the dinosaur when it stood up from a resting position (see diagrams opposite).

The scene below shows Albertosaurus about to catch Corythosaurus, a herbivore which it often hunted. Corythosaurus was a hadrosaur (see pages 28-29).

Shoulder bone

Large openings in skull

Teeth

Skin

Ribs

Muscle

Digits

Forearm bone

Thigh bone

Leg bones

Digits

Claws

CORYTHOSAURUS 10 metres long 92-72 million years ago

Although the tyrannosaurs were large, most dinosaur experts believe that they could move quite fast. The massive tail balanced the body and head and the long back legs enabled the dinosaur to run with great, loping strides. However, its great weight would have prevented it running long distances and it probably ambushed its prey so that the chase before the kill was as short as possible.

CARNIVOROUS DINOSAURS
THE NIMBLE MEAT-EATERS

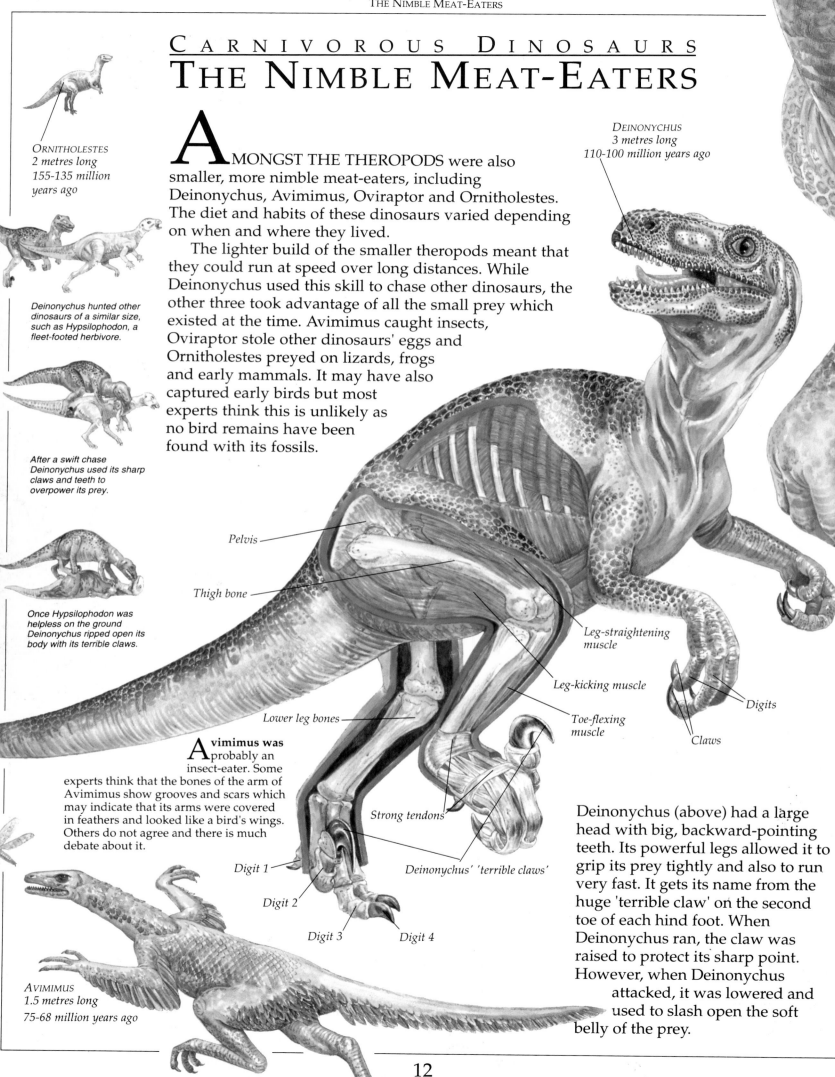

AMONGST THE THEROPODS were also smaller, more nimble meat-eaters, including Deinonychus, Avimimus, Oviraptor and Ornitholestes. The diet and habits of these dinosaurs varied depending on when and where they lived.

The lighter build of the smaller theropods meant that they could run at speed over long distances. While Deinonychus used this skill to chase other dinosaurs, the other three took advantage of all the small prey which existed at the time. Avimimus caught insects, Oviraptor stole other dinosaurs' eggs and Ornitholestes preyed on lizards, frogs and early mammals. It may have also captured early birds but most experts think this is unlikely as no bird remains have been found with its fossils.

ORNITHOLESTES
2 metres long
155-135 million years ago

Deinonychus hunted other dinosaurs of a similar size, such as Hypsilophodon, a fleet-footed herbivore.

After a swift chase Deinonychus used its sharp claws and teeth to overpower its prey.

Once Hypsilophodon was helpless on the ground Deinonychus ripped open its body with its terrible claws.

DEINONYCHUS
3 metres long
110-100 million years ago

Pelvis

Thigh bone

Leg-straightening muscle

Leg-kicking muscle

Toe-flexing muscle

Digits

Claws

Lower leg bones

Avimimus was probably an insect-eater. Some experts think that the bones of the arm of Avimimus show grooves and scars which may indicate that its arms were covered in feathers and looked like a bird's wings. Others do not agree and there is much debate about it.

Strong tendons

Digit 1

Digit 2

Digit 3

Digit 4

Deinonychus' 'terrible claws'

Deinonychus (above) had a large head with big, backward-pointing teeth. Its powerful legs allowed it to grip its prey tightly and also to run very fast. It gets its name from the huge 'terrible claw' on the second toe of each hind foot. When Deinonychus ran, the claw was raised to protect its sharp point. However, when Deinonychus attacked, it was lowered and used to slash open the soft belly of the prey.

AVIMIMUS
1.5 metres long
75-68 million years ago

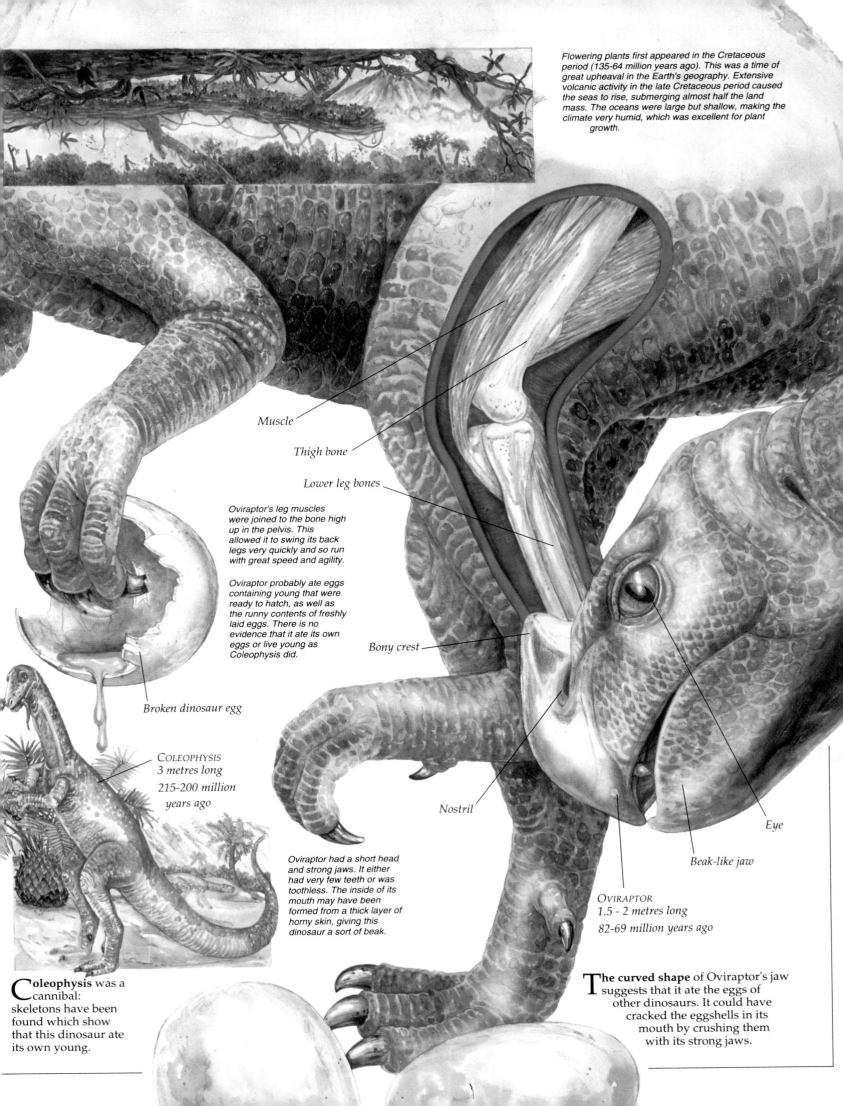

Flowering plants first appeared in the Cretaceous period (135-64 million years ago). This was a time of great upheaval in the Earth's geography. Extensive volcanic activity in the late Cretaceous period caused the seas to rise, submerging almost half the land mass. The oceans were large but shallow, making the climate very humid, which was excellent for plant growth.

Muscle

Thigh bone

Lower leg bones

Oviraptor's leg muscles were joined to the bone high up in the pelvis. This allowed it to swing its back legs very quickly and so run with great speed and agility.

Oviraptor probably ate eggs containing young that were ready to hatch, as well as the runny contents of freshly laid eggs. There is no evidence that it ate its own eggs or live young as Coleophysis did.

Bony crest

Broken dinosaur egg

COLEOPHYSIS
3 metres long
215-200 million
years ago

Nostril

Oviraptor had a short head and strong jaws. It either had very few teeth or was toothless. The inside of its mouth may have been formed from a thick layer of horny skin, giving this dinosaur a sort of beak.

Eye

Beak-like jaw

OVIRAPTOR
1.5 - 2 metres long
82-69 million years ago

Coleophysis was a cannibal: skeletons have been found which show that this dinosaur ate its own young.

The curved shape of Oviraptor's jaw suggests that it ate the eggs of other dinosaurs. It could have cracked the eggshells in its mouth by crushing them with its strong jaws.

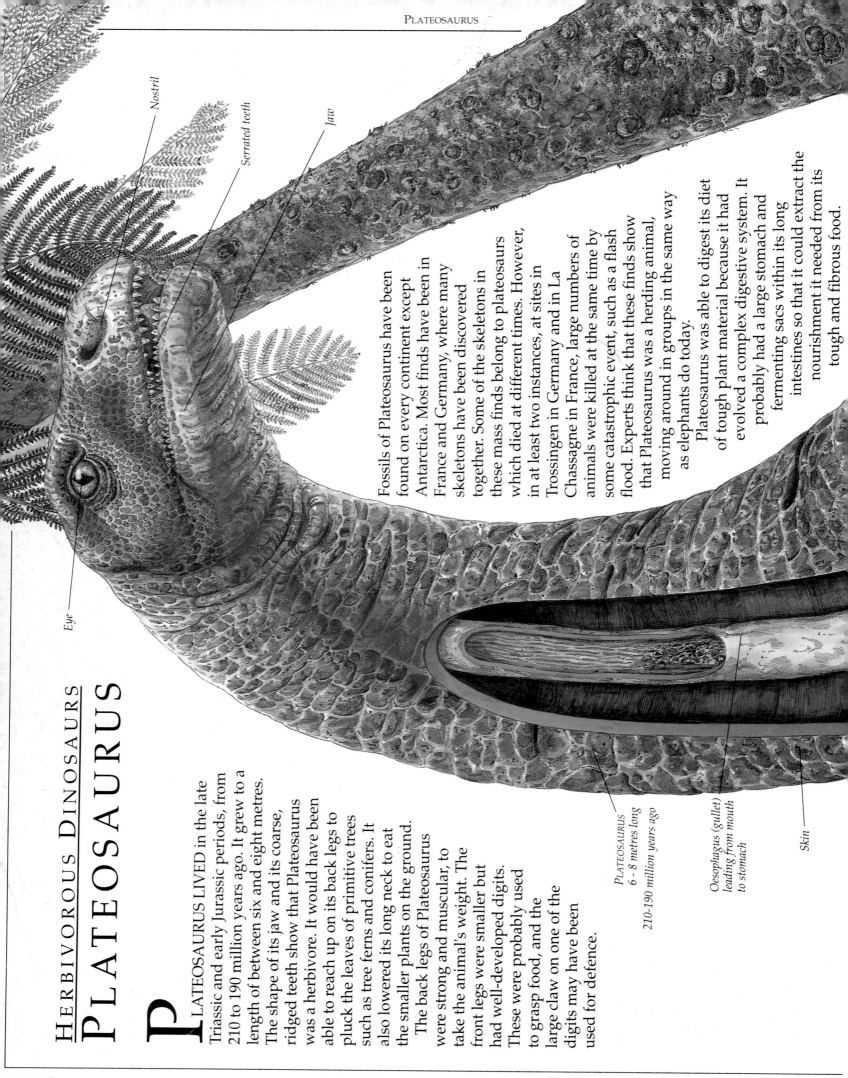

Nostril

Serrated teeth

Jaw

Eye

HERBIVOROUS DINOSAURS
PLATEOSAURUS

PLATEOSAURUS LIVED in the late Triassic and early Jurassic periods, from 210 to 190 million years ago. It grew to a length of between six and eight metres. The shape of its jaw and its coarse, ridged teeth show that Plateosaurus was a herbivore. It would have been able to reach up on its back legs to pluck the leaves of primitive trees such as tree ferns and conifers. It also lowered its long neck to eat the smaller plants on the ground.

The back legs of Plateosaurus were strong and muscular, to take the animal's weight. The front legs were smaller but had well-developed digits. These were probably used to grasp food, and the large claw on one of the digits may have been used for defence.

Fossils of Plateosaurus have been found on every continent except Antarctica. Most finds have been in France and Germany, where many skeletons have been discovered together. Some of the skeletons in these mass finds belong to plateosaurs which died at different times. However, in at least two instances, at sites in Trossingen in Germany and in La Chassagne in France, large numbers of animals were killed at the same time by some catastrophic event, such as a flash flood. Experts think that these finds show that Plateosaurus was a herding animal, moving around in groups in the same way as elephants do today.

Plateosaurus was able to digest its diet of tough plant material because it had evolved a complex digestive system. It probably had a large stomach and fermenting sacs within its long intestines so that it could extract the nourishment it needed from its tough and fibrous food.

PLATEOSAURUS
6 – 8 metres long
210-190 million years ago

Oesophagus (gullet)
leading from mouth
to stomach

Skin

Muscle

Upper arm bone

Lower arm bones

Ribs

Digit 1

Claws

Digit 2

Digit 3

Digit 4

Digit 5

Gastroliths

Stomach

Stomach wall

Intestines

Fermenting chambers

A Plateosaurus herd

The **stomach** of Plateosaurus is thought to have contained a large number of stones (gastroliths). Lodged in the wall of the stomach, these stones were probably quite large and heavy. They were used to grind the branches, twigs and leaves the animal had eaten into a fine pulp ready for digestion.

The **gastroliths** which have been discovered are about 10 centimetres long.

Large **dinosaur** herds may have been better at fending off predators than single dinosaurs. Plateosaurus may have lived in family groups which were, in turn, part of a larger herd.

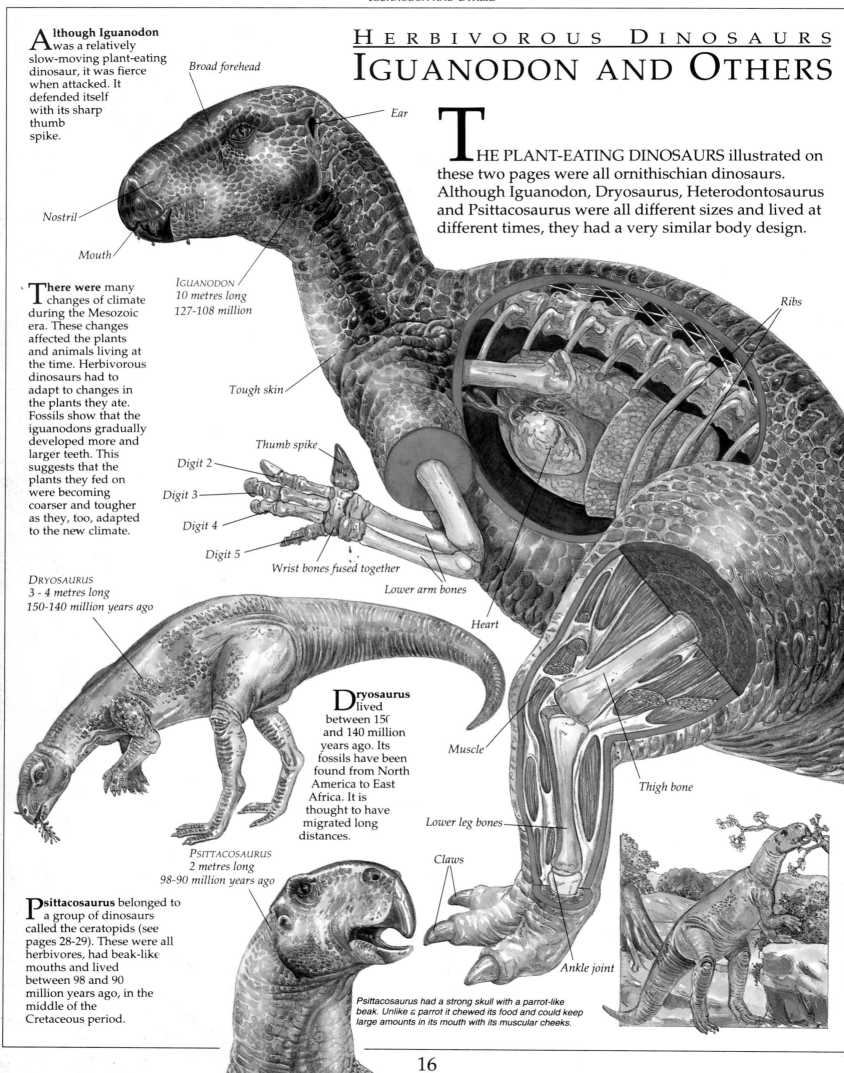

Although **Iguanodon** was a relatively slow-moving plant-eating dinosaur, it was fierce when attacked. It defended itself with its sharp thumb spike.

Broad forehead

Ear

Nostril

Mouth

HERBIVOROUS DINOSAURS
IGUANODON AND OTHERS

THE PLANT-EATING DINOSAURS illustrated on these two pages were all ornithischian dinosaurs. Although Iguanodon, Dryosaurus, Heterodontosaurus and Psittacosaurus were all different sizes and lived at different times, they had a very similar body design.

There were many changes of climate during the Mesozoic era. These changes affected the plants and animals living at the time. Herbivorous dinosaurs had to adapt to changes in the plants they ate. Fossils show that the iguanodons gradually developed more and larger teeth. This suggests that the plants they fed on were becoming coarser and tougher as they, too, adapted to the new climate.

*IGUANODON
10 metres long
127-108 million*

Ribs

Tough skin

Thumb spike

Digit 2

Digit 3

Digit 4

Digit 5

Wrist bones fused together

Lower arm bones

Heart

*DRYOSAURUS
3 - 4 metres long
150-140 million years ago*

Dryosaurus lived between 150 and 140 million years ago. Its fossils have been found from North America to East Africa. It is thought to have migrated long distances.

Muscle

Thigh bone

Lower leg bones

Claws

Ankle joint

*PSITTACOSAURUS
2 metres long
98-90 million years ago*

Psittacosaurus belonged to a group of dinosaurs called the ceratopids (see pages 28-29). These were all herbivores, had beak-like mouths and lived between 98 and 90 million years ago, in the middle of the Cretaceous period.

Psittacosaurus had a strong skull with a parrot-like beak. Unlike a parrot it chewed its food and could keep large amounts in its mouth with its muscular cheeks.

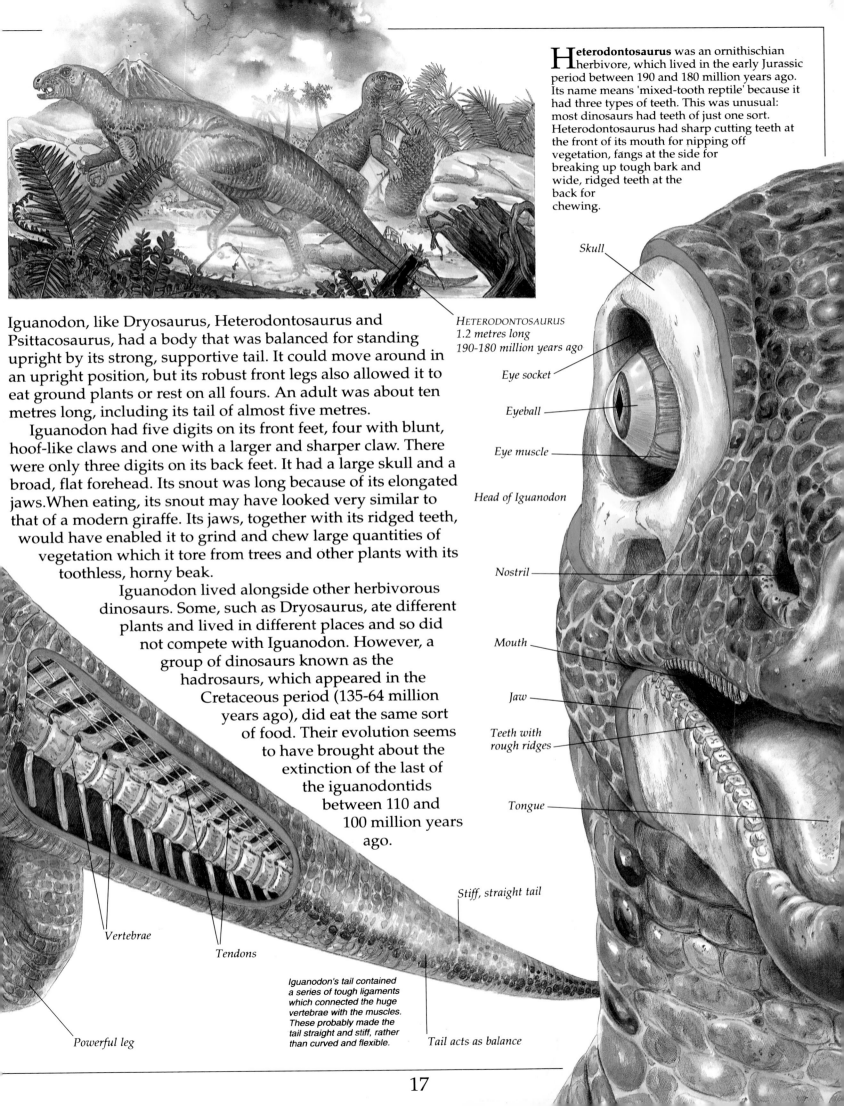

Heterodontosaurus was an ornithischian herbivore, which lived in the early Jurassic period between 190 and 180 million years ago. Its name means 'mixed-tooth reptile' because it had three types of teeth. This was unusual: most dinosaurs had teeth of just one sort. Heterodontosaurus had sharp cutting teeth at the front of its mouth for nipping off vegetation, fangs at the side for breaking up tough bark and wide, ridged teeth at the back for chewing.

HETERODONTOSAURUS
1.2 metres long
190-180 million years ago

Skull

Eye socket

Eyeball

Eye muscle

Head of Iguanodon

Nostril

Mouth

Jaw

Teeth with rough ridges

Tongue

Iguanodon, like Dryosaurus, Heterodontosaurus and Psittacosaurus, had a body that was balanced for standing upright by its strong, supportive tail. It could move around in an upright position, but its robust front legs also allowed it to eat ground plants or rest on all fours. An adult was about ten metres long, including its tail of almost five metres.

Iguanodon had five digits on its front feet, four with blunt, hoof-like claws and one with a larger and sharper claw. There were only three digits on its back feet. It had a large skull and a broad, flat forehead. Its snout was long because of its elongated jaws. When eating, its snout may have looked very similar to that of a modern giraffe. Its jaws, together with its ridged teeth, would have enabled it to grind and chew large quantities of vegetation which it tore from trees and other plants with its toothless, horny beak.

Iguanodon lived alongside other herbivorous dinosaurs. Some, such as Dryosaurus, ate different plants and lived in different places and so did not compete with Iguanodon. However, a group of dinosaurs known as the hadrosaurs, which appeared in the Cretaceous period (135-64 million years ago), did eat the same sort of food. Their evolution seems to have brought about the extinction of the last of the iguanodontids between 110 and 100 million years ago.

Vertebrae

Tendons

Stiff, straight tail

Iguanodon's tail contained a series of tough ligaments which connected the huge vertebrae with the muscles. These probably made the tail straight and stiff, rather than curved and flexible.

Powerful leg

Tail acts as balance

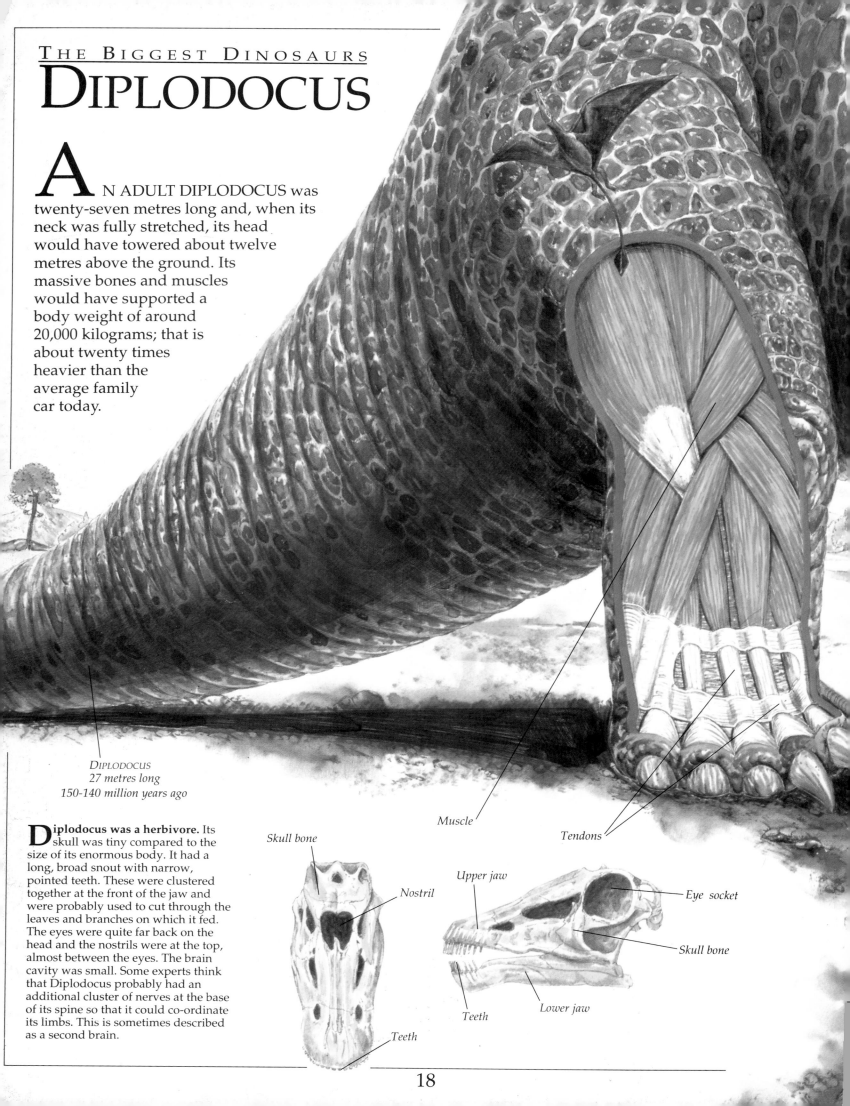

DIPLODOCUS

A N ADULT DIPLODOCUS was twenty-seven metres long and, when its neck was fully stretched, its head would have towered about twelve metres above the ground. Its massive bones and muscles would have supported a body weight of around 20,000 kilograms; that is about twenty times heavier than the average family car today.

DIPLODOCUS
27 metres long
150-140 million years ago

Diplodocus was a herbivore. Its skull was tiny compared to the size of its enormous body. It had a long, broad snout with narrow, pointed teeth. These were clustered together at the front of the jaw and were probably used to cut through the leaves and branches on which it fed. The eyes were quite far back on the head and the nostrils were at the top, almost between the eyes. The brain cavity was small. Some experts think that Diplodocus probably had an additional cluster of nerves at the base of its spine so that it could co-ordinate its limbs. This is sometimes described as a second brain.

Muscle

Tendons

Skull bone

Nostril

Upper jaw

Eye socket

Skull bone

Teeth

Lower jaw

Teeth

Muscle

Tendons

Diplodocus fossils were first found in Colorado in the USA in 1877. Since then many skeletons have been found in North America, particularly in Colorado and Wyoming. All date from the late Jurassic period, between 148 and 138 million years ago. Diplodocus had 15 neck vertebrae, 10 back vertebrae and 73 tail vertebrae. The bones of the legs were very thick to carry the weight of the animal and to support its massive muscles.

Diplodocus reproduced by laying eggs. Only fragments of these have been found but they are thought to have been tiny in comparison to the parent; no more than a few centimetres long. The young must have grown very quickly or they would have been killed and eaten by predators.

The **skull bones** of Brachiosaurus were quite thin, with air spaces between them, so reducing the weight of the head. Even so, the neck vertebrae had to be very large to support the dinosaur's long neck.

Bony crest

The crest on the top of Brachiosaurus' head was formed by the large space occupied by its nostrils. Such large nostrils may have given Brachiosaurus a good sense of smell.

THE BIGGEST DINOSAURS
OTHER DINOSAUR GIANTS

THE LATE JURASSIC PERIOD (from about 150 to 135 million years ago) was the age of the biggest dinosaurs. As well as Diplodocus (pages 18 and 19), Apatosaurus (twenty-one metres long), Brachiosaurus (twenty-seven metres long) and Camarasaurus (eighteen metres long) roamed the Jurassic landscape.

Apatosaurus, also known as Brontosaurus, was more heavily built than Diplodocus, weighing about 30,000 kilograms. Brachiosaurus, although the same length as Diplodocus, weighed an enormous 80,000 kilograms.

All of these giant dinosaurs were herbivores and had to eat vast amounts of plant material to maintain their size. Their long necks enabled them to stretch up to the tops of trees which smaller dinosaurs could not reach. In comparison, the largest carnivorous dinosaurs, Tyrannosaurus (fourteen metres long) and Allosaurus (twelve metres long) seemed small.

APATOSAURUS
21 metres long
150-125 million years ago

BRACHIOSAURUS
27 metres long
150-125 million years ago

The limbs of Apatosaurus were pillar-like to support its great weight. Its feet would probably have looked like those of a modern elephant.

Apatosaurus was a relative of Diplodocus, with a similar body shape and habitat. The skeleton of Apatosaurus was more robust, with thicker vertebrae and sturdier leg and pelvic bones. Both dinosaurs probably had gastroliths (stomach stones) like Plateosaurus (see pages 14 - 15) to grind up the plant material that they ate so that it could be digested more easily.

Apart from its enormous bulk another distinctive feature of Brachiosaurus was its extremely long neck which measured about 9 metres. Brachiosaurus also had front legs which were longer than its back legs.

Allosaurus, one of the large carnivorous theropods, lived in North America between 150 and 125 million years ago. Its huge head, with rows of dagger-like teeth, was almost a metre long. Even so, it was much smaller than the giant herbivorous dinosaurs shown here.

ALLOSAURUS
12 metres long
150-125 million years ago

Experts have recently suggested that long-necked dinosaurs may have had as many as 8 hearts to enable them to pump blood up to their brains. There may have been 2 main hearts in the chest and 3 pairs of smaller ones in the neck itself.

Nostril

Camarasaurus was similar in body shape to Brachiosaurus but was smaller. It had a short skull with a wide nose and its nostrils were positioned on the top of its head. The reason for this is not known.

Muscle

Ribs

CAMARASAURUS
18 metres long
150-125 million years ago

Neck vertebrae

Bony plates in skin

Eye

Leathery skin

THE SMALLEST DINOSAURS
SMALL DINOSAURS OF THE EARLY JURASSIC

BETWEEN 200 AND 180 MILLION YEARS AGO three successful small dinosaurs, Lesothosaurus, Scutellosaurus and Segisaurus, moved through the early Jurassic landscape.

Lesothosaurus grew to a length of about ninety centimetres. It was lightly built and moved around at high speed on its muscular back legs. It used its front limbs to gather leaves and other plant material which it chewed with its sharp, serrated teeth. Scutellosaurus was a close relative of Lesothosaurus. It was about 130 centimetres long, with an extremely long, thin tail. A series of bony plates were set into the skin along its back. Although its front legs were shorter than its back ones, they were quite sturdy, so it could move around on all fours, unlike its relative Lesothosaurus. Segisaurus grew to be about one metre long. A small and agile runner, it probably ate small lizards and amphibians.

LESOTHOSAURUS
0.9 metres long
200-190 million
years ago

SCUTELLOSAURUS
1.3 metres long
198-190 million years ago

Scutellosaurus was not quite as fast-moving as Lesothosaurus. As it could not out-run its predators it adopted another defensive strategy to compensate. Like the armadillo of today, it had bony plates buried in its thick, leathery skin to protect it from the teeth and claws of predators. The plates would also have made it a very unappetising meal. The disadvantage of such plates was weight; the heavier the plates, the slower the animal.

Few Segisaurus fossils have ever been found. The little we know about this dinosaur comes from several broken skeletons which were found in the Segi Canyon, Arizona, USA, during the 1930s.

Cycad

Lesothosaurus gets its name from the river Lesotho in southern Africa, where one of the best-preserved skeletons was discovered. The skull had a cavity just behind the nostril which may have contained a salt gland when the animal was alive. This could indicate that Lesothosaurus lived in hot, dry conditions. In such conditions animals need to control the salt content of their bodies. During droughts the salt gland helps them to dispose of excess body salts which would harm them if they remained in the body.

*SEGISAURUS
1 metre long
190-180 million years ago*

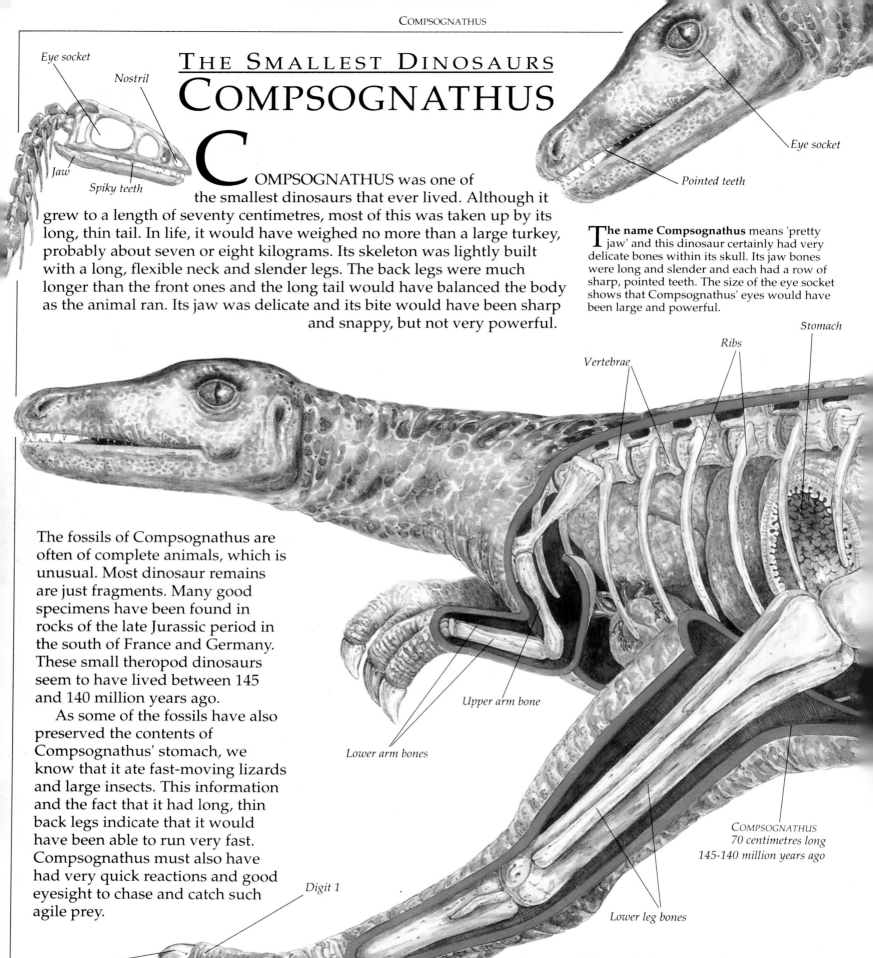

Eye socket

Nostril

Jaw

Spiky teeth

Eye socket

Pointed teeth

THE SMALLEST DINOSAURS
COMPSOGNATHUS

COMPSOGNATHUS was one of the smallest dinosaurs that ever lived. Although it grew to a length of seventy centimetres, most of this was taken up by its long, thin tail. In life, it would have weighed no more than a large turkey, probably about seven or eight kilograms. Its skeleton was lightly built with a long, flexible neck and slender legs. The back legs were much longer than the front ones and the long tail would have balanced the body as the animal ran. Its jaw was delicate and its bite would have been sharp and snappy, but not very powerful.

The name Compsognathus means 'pretty jaw' and this dinosaur certainly had very delicate bones within its skull. Its jaw bones were long and slender and each had a row of sharp, pointed teeth. The size of the eye socket shows that Compsognathus' eyes would have been large and powerful.

Stomach

Ribs

Vertebrae

The fossils of Compsognathus are often of complete animals, which is unusual. Most dinosaur remains are just fragments. Many good specimens have been found in rocks of the late Jurassic period in the south of France and Germany. These small theropod dinosaurs seem to have lived between 145 and 140 million years ago.

As some of the fossils have also preserved the contents of Compsognathus' stomach, we know that it ate fast-moving lizards and large insects. This information and the fact that it had long, thin back legs indicate that it would have been able to run very fast. Compsognathus must also have had very quick reactions and good eyesight to chase and catch such agile prey.

Upper arm bone

Lower arm bones

Digit 1

Claws

Digit 2

Digit 3

Digit 4

COMPSOGNATHUS
70 centimetres long
145-140 million years ago

Lower leg bones

The neck of Compsognathus was strong and flexible, enabling it to make rapid, darting movements with its head. This would have been important for catching fast-moving prey. Fossil skeletons show the neck arched back over the spine. This was probably caused by the neck muscles going into spasm after death

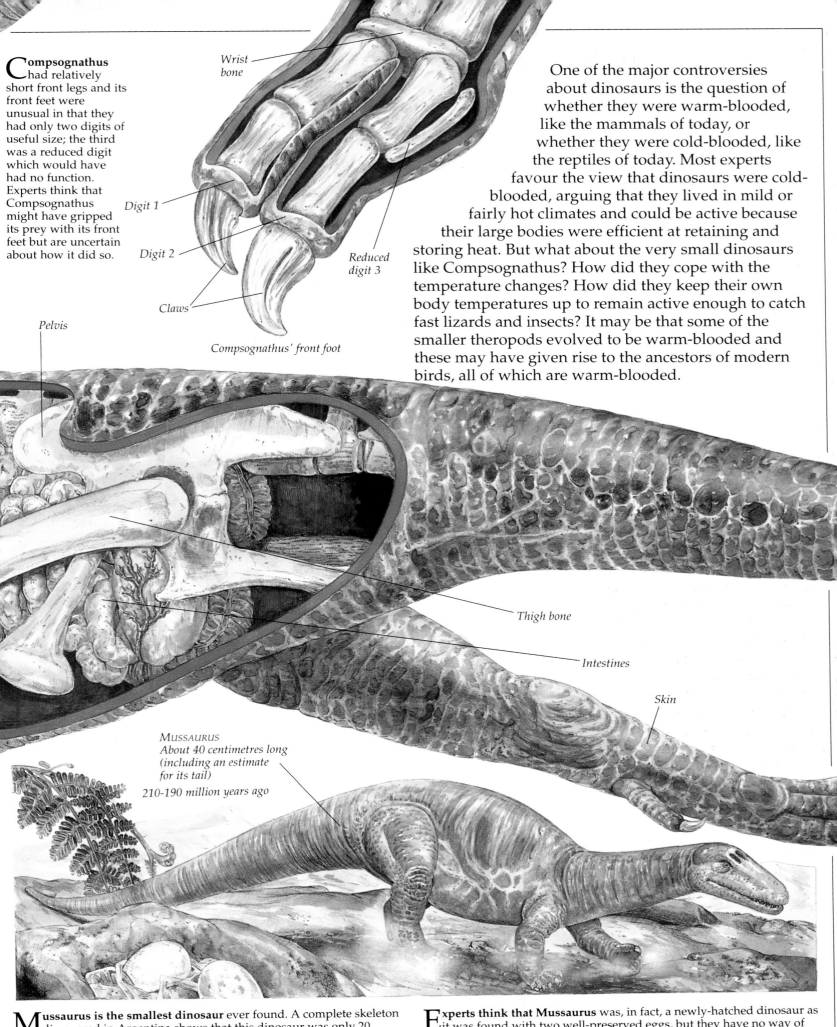

Compsognathus had relatively short front legs and its front feet were unusual in that they had only two digits of useful size; the third was a reduced digit which would have had no function. Experts think that Compsognathus might have gripped its prey with its front feet but are uncertain about how it did so.

Wrist bone

Digit 1

Digit 2

Reduced digit 3

Claws

Pelvis

Compsognathus' front foot

One of the major controversies about dinosaurs is the question of whether they were warm-blooded, like the mammals of today, or whether they were cold-blooded, like the reptiles of today. Most experts favour the view that dinosaurs were cold-blooded, arguing that they lived in mild or fairly hot climates and could be active because their large bodies were efficient at retaining and storing heat. But what about the very small dinosaurs like Compsognathus? How did they cope with the temperature changes? How did they keep their own body temperatures up to remain active enough to catch fast lizards and insects? It may be that some of the smaller theropods evolved to be warm-blooded and these may have given rise to the ancestors of modern birds, all of which are warm-blooded.

Thigh bone

Intestines

Skin

MUSSAURUS
About 40 centimetres long (including an estimate for its tail)
210-190 million years ago

Mussaurus is the smallest dinosaur ever found. A complete skeleton discovered in Argentina shows that this dinosaur was only 20 centimetres long from its head to the base of its tail.

Experts think that Mussaurus was, in fact, a newly-hatched dinosaur as it was found with two well-preserved eggs, but they have no way of knowing how big an adult Mussaurus would have been.

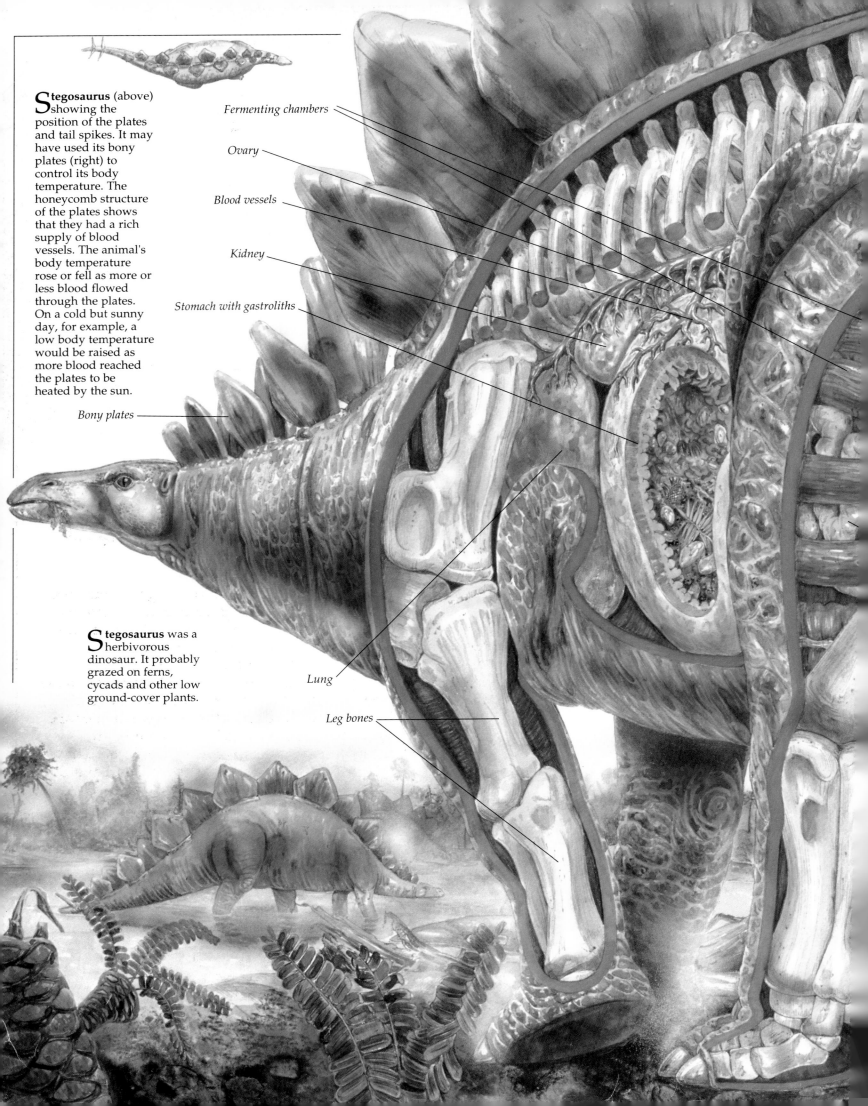

Stegosaurus (above) showing the position of the plates and tail spikes. It may have used its bony plates (right) to control its body temperature. The honeycomb structure of the plates shows that they had a rich supply of blood vessels. The animal's body temperature rose or fell as more or less blood flowed through the plates. On a cold but sunny day, for example, a low body temperature would be raised as more blood reached the plates to be heated by the sun.

Bony plates —

Stegosaurus was a herbivorous dinosaur. It probably grazed on ferns, cycads and other low ground-cover plants.

Fermenting chambers

Ovary

Blood vessels

Kidney

Stomach with gastroliths —

Lung

Leg bones

Vertebrae

Pelvis

Thigh bone

STEGOSAURUS
6 - 7.5 metres long
150-140 million years ago

Intestines

ARMOUR-PLATED DINOSAURS
STEGOSAURUS

STEGOSAURUS LIVED 150 to 140 million years ago. Its massive body was supported by strong, pillar-like legs. Its head and brain were tiny in comparison to the size of its body. An adult of 1500 kilograms had a brain which weighed only seventy to eighty grams.

Bony plates, about sixty or seventy centimetres high and fifty centimetres wide, grew in a staggered pattern along Stegosaurus' back. They were probably used to control body temperature (see page 26). The plates at the base of the tail were thinner and their sharp points could have been used in defence. Stegosaurus, when attacked, could have whipped its tail and used the spiked end as a club.

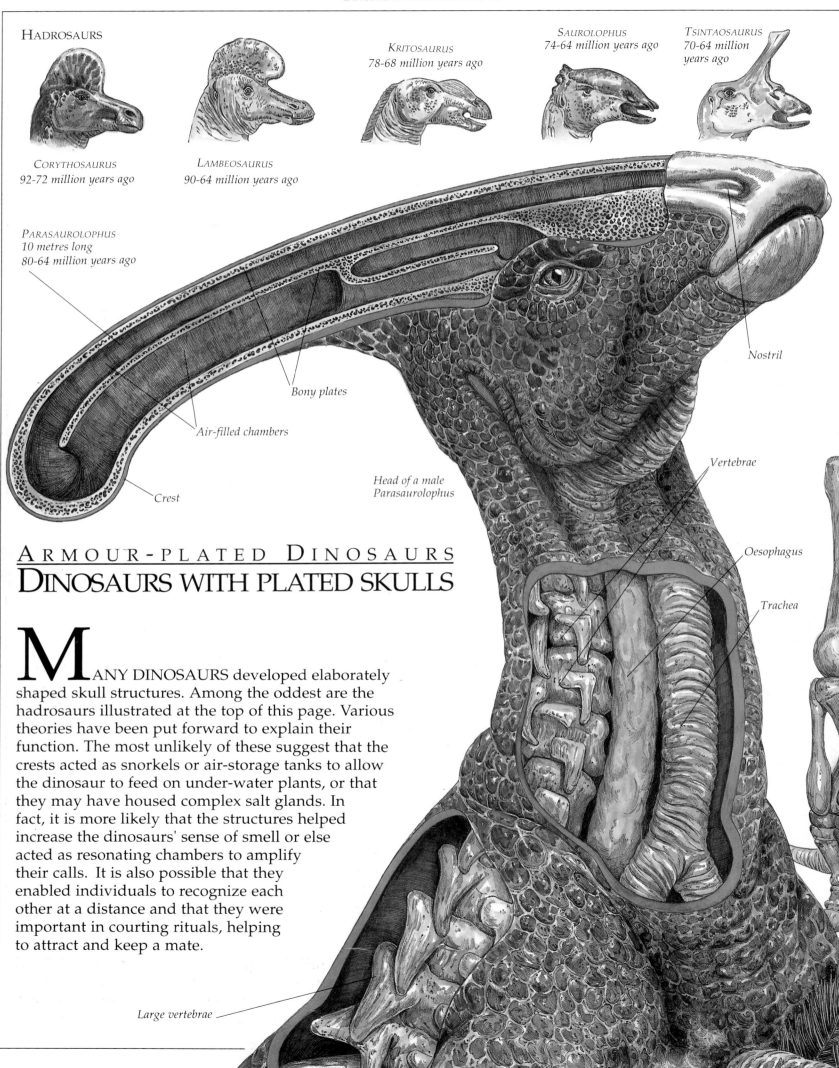

HADROSAURS

CORYTHOSAURUS
92-72 million years ago

LAMBEOSAURUS
90-64 million years ago

KRITOSAURUS
78-68 million years ago

SAUROLOPHUS
74-64 million years ago

TSINTAOSAURUS
70-64 million years ago

PARASAUROLOPHUS
10 metres long
80-64 million years ago

Bony plates

Air-filled chambers

Crest

Head of a male
Parasaurolophus

Nostril

Vertebrae

Oesophagus

Trachea

Large vertebrae

ARMOUR-PLATED DINOSAURS
DINOSAURS WITH PLATED SKULLS

MANY DINOSAURS developed elaborately shaped skull structures. Among the oddest are the hadrosaurs illustrated at the top of this page. Various theories have been put forward to explain their function. The most unlikely of these suggest that the crests acted as snorkels or air-storage tanks to allow the dinosaur to feed on under-water plants, or that they may have housed complex salt glands. In fact, it is more likely that the structures helped increase the dinosaurs' sense of smell or else acted as resonating chambers to amplify their calls. It is also possible that they enabled individuals to recognize each other at a distance and that they were important in courting rituals, helping to attract and keep a mate.

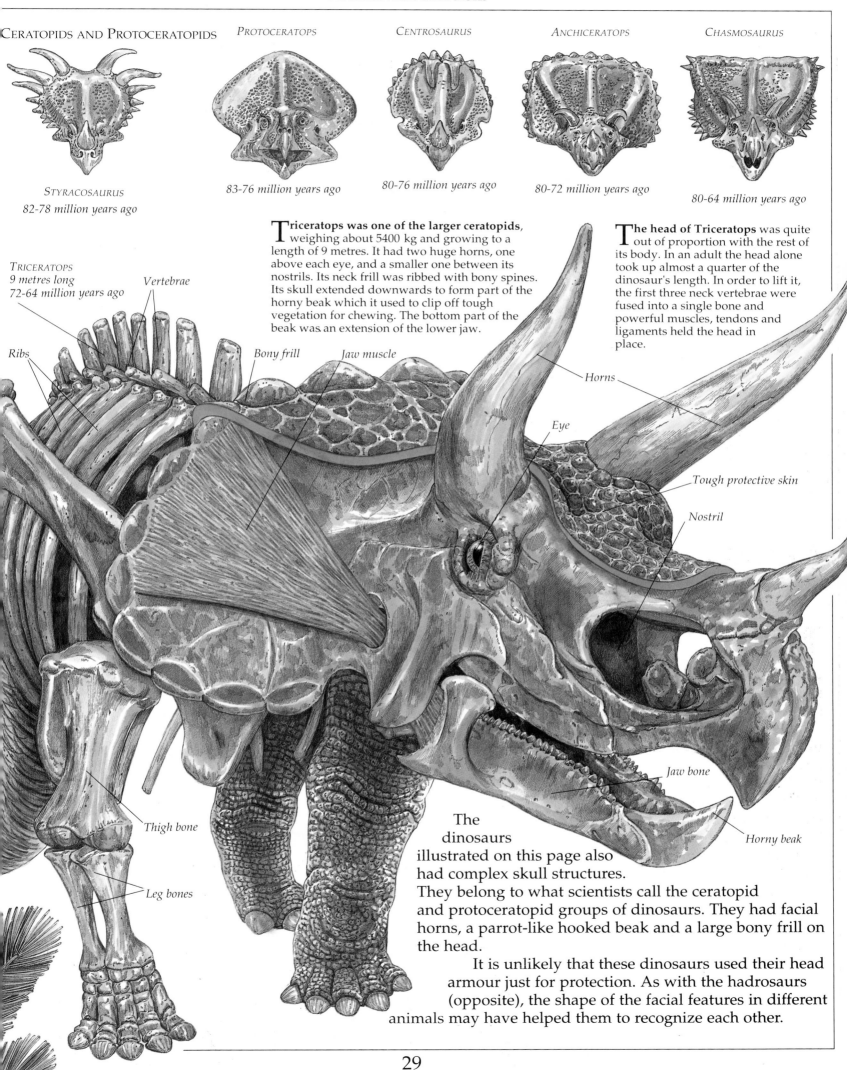

CERATOPIDS AND PROTOCERATOPIDS

STYRACOSAURUS
82-78 million years ago

PROTOCERATOPS
83-76 million years ago

CENTROSAURUS
80-76 million years ago

ANCHICERATOPS
80-72 million years ago

CHASMOSAURUS
80-64 million years ago

Triceratops was one of the larger ceratopids, weighing about 5400 kg and growing to a length of 9 metres. It had two huge horns, one above each eye, and a smaller one between its nostrils. Its neck frill was ribbed with bony spines. Its skull extended downwards to form part of the horny beak which it used to clip off tough vegetation for chewing. The bottom part of the beak was an extension of the lower jaw.

The head of Triceratops was quite out of proportion with the rest of its body. In an adult the head alone took up almost a quarter of the dinosaur's length. In order to lift it, the first three neck vertebrae were fused into a single bone and powerful muscles, tendons and ligaments held the head in place.

TRICERATOPS
9 metres long
72-64 million years ago

Vertebrae

Ribs

Bony frill

Jaw muscle

Horns

Eye

Tough protective skin

Nostril

Jaw bone

Thigh bone

Leg bones

Horny beak

The dinosaurs illustrated on this page also had complex skull structures.
They belong to what scientists call the ceratopid and protoceratopid groups of dinosaurs. They had facial horns, a parrot-like hooked beak and a large bony frill on the head.

It is unlikely that these dinosaurs used their head armour just for protection. As with the hadrosaurs (opposite), the shape of the facial features in different animals may have helped them to recognize each other.

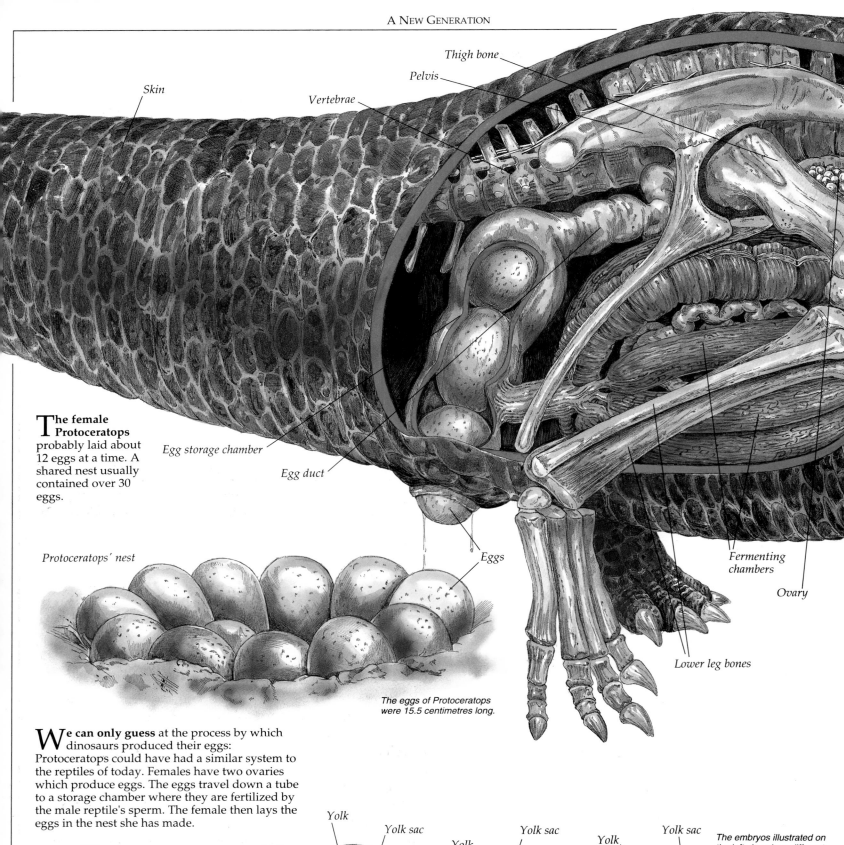

Skin

Vertebrae

Thigh bone

Pelvis

Egg storage chamber

Egg duct

Eggs

Fermenting chambers

Ovary

Lower leg bones

The female **Protoceratops** probably laid about 12 eggs at a time. A shared nest usually contained over 30 eggs.

Protoceratops' nest

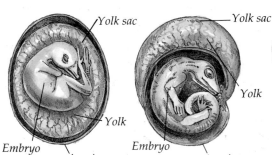

The eggs of Protoceratops were 15.5 centimetres long.

We can only guess at the process by which dinosaurs produced their eggs: Protoceratops could have had a similar system to the reptiles of today. Females have two ovaries which produce eggs. The eggs travel down a tube to a storage chamber where they are fertilized by the male reptile's sperm. The female then lays the eggs in the nest she has made.

Yolk sac

Yolk

Embryo

Amnion

Bird embryo

Yolk sac

Yolk

Embryo

Amnion

Lizard embryo

Yolk

Yolk sac

Embryo

Amnion

Crocodile embryo

Yolk sac

Yolk

Embryo

Amnion

Turtle embryo

Yolk

Yolk sac

Embryo

Amnion

Mammal embryo

The embryos illustrated on the left show how different animals look when they first start to develop. All the embryos have features showing which animal they will grow into, although they do look very similar at first glance. The membranes and yolk which surround them are all formed in much the same way. The bird, lizard, crocodile and turtle embryos are all contained within the shell of an egg, just as a dinosaur embryo was. The embryos of mammals, including humans, grow without a shell and develop inside their mothers' bodies.

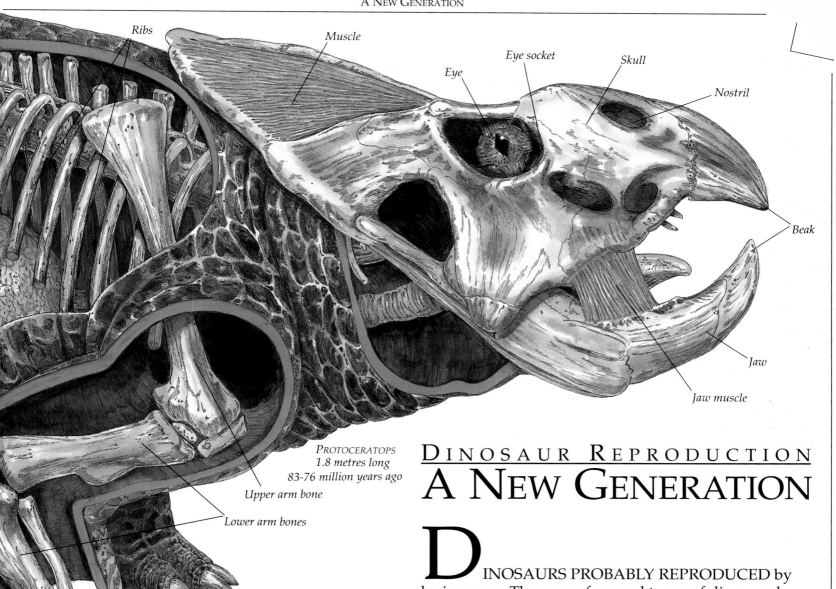

Ribs

Muscle

Eye

Eye socket

Skull

Nostril

Beak

Jaw

Jaw muscle

PROTOCERATOPS
1.8 metres long
83-76 million years ago

Upper arm bone

Lower arm bones

Digits

Claws

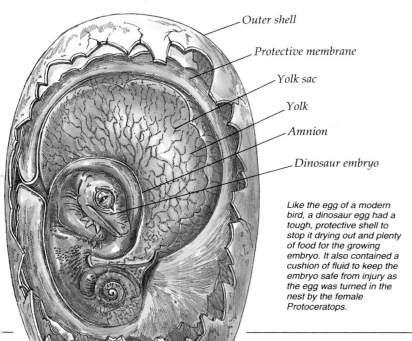

Outer shell

Protective membrane

Yolk sac

Yolk

Amnion

Dinosaur embryo

Like the egg of a modern bird, a dinosaur egg had a tough, protective shell to stop it drying out and plenty of food for the growing embryo. It also contained a cushion of fluid to keep the embryo safe from injury as the egg was turned in the nest by the female Protoceratops.

DINOSAUR REPRODUCTION
A NEW GENERATION

DINOSAURS PROBABLY REPRODUCED by laying eggs. The eggs of several types of dinosaur have been found, but the best-preserved are in nests of Protoceratops and Maiasaura (see pages 32-33).

In the 1920s an expedition to the Gobi Desert in Mongolia discovered one of the most amazing collections of dinosaur skeletons ever found. At one site there were many complete skeletons of Protoceratops. The remains included young dinosaurs which had probably just hatched, together with undisturbed nests of unhatched eggs.

These remains suggest that the mother Protoceratops would carefully scoop out a nest in the sand and then lay her eggs in a ring, with their narrow ends pointing inwards. Several nests were found in the same area, suggesting that many females used the same breeding ground. They may even have shared the same nests, taking it in turns to incubate the eggs and sharing the care of the tiny hatchlings. A large, shared nesting site would also have been safer. Oviraptors, which lived 82-69 million years ago, certainly ate the eggs of Protoceratops which lived between 83 and 76 million years ago. One fossilized Oviraptor, with a badly crushed skull, has been found on top of a clutch of Protoceratops eggs, perhaps caught in the act of stealing them by an irate parent.

DINOSAUR REPRODUCTION
THE NEST COMES TO LIFE

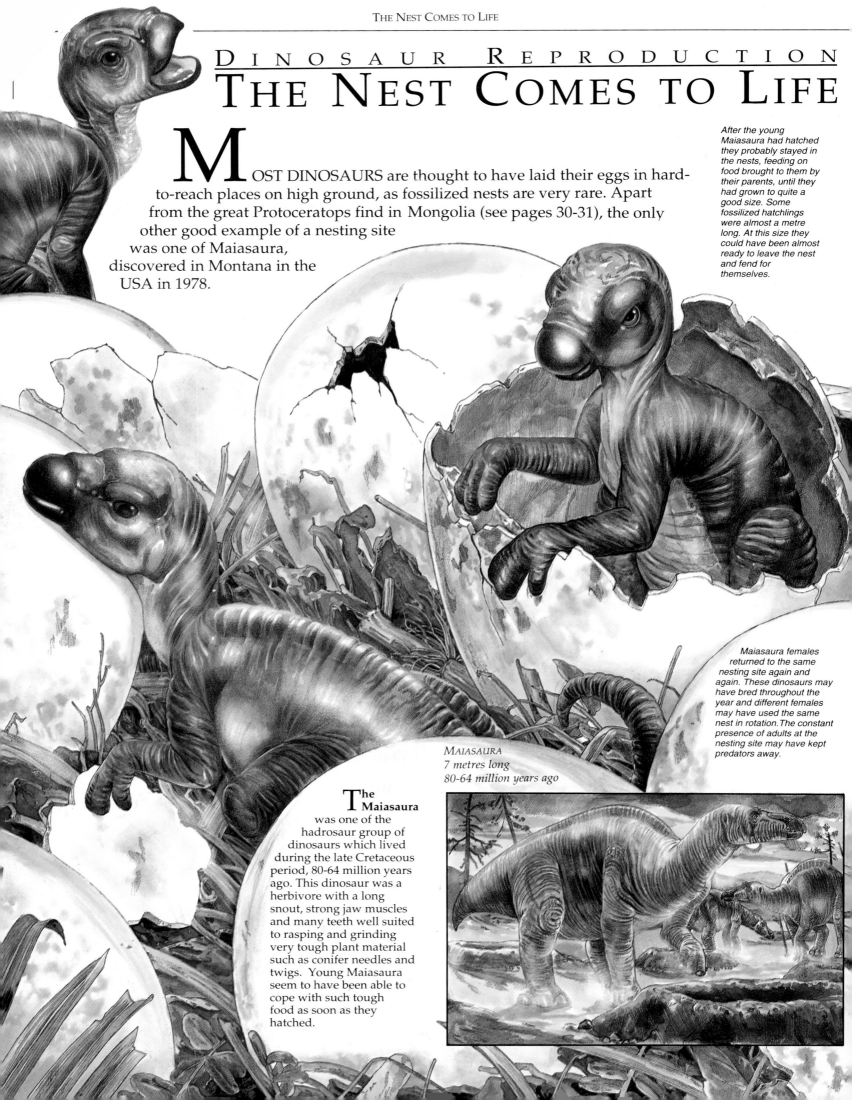

MOST DINOSAURS are thought to have laid their eggs in hard-to-reach places on high ground, as fossilized nests are very rare. Apart from the great Protoceratops find in Mongolia (see pages 30-31), the only other good example of a nesting site was one of Maiasaura, discovered in Montana in the USA in 1978.

After the young Maiasaura had hatched they probably stayed in the nests, feeding on food brought to them by their parents, until they had grown to quite a good size. Some fossilized hatchlings were almost a metre long. At this size they could have been almost ready to leave the nest and fend for themselves.

Maiasaura females returned to the same nesting site again and again. These dinosaurs may have bred throughout the year and different females may have used the same nest in rotation. The constant presence of adults at the nesting site may have kept predators away.

MAIASAURA
7 metres long
80-64 million years ago

The **Maiasaura** was one of the hadrosaur group of dinosaurs which lived during the late Cretaceous period, 80-64 million years ago. This dinosaur was a herbivore with a long snout, strong jaw muscles and many teeth well suited to rasping and grinding very tough plant material such as conifer needles and twigs. Young Maiasaura seem to have been able to cope with such tough food as soon as they hatched.

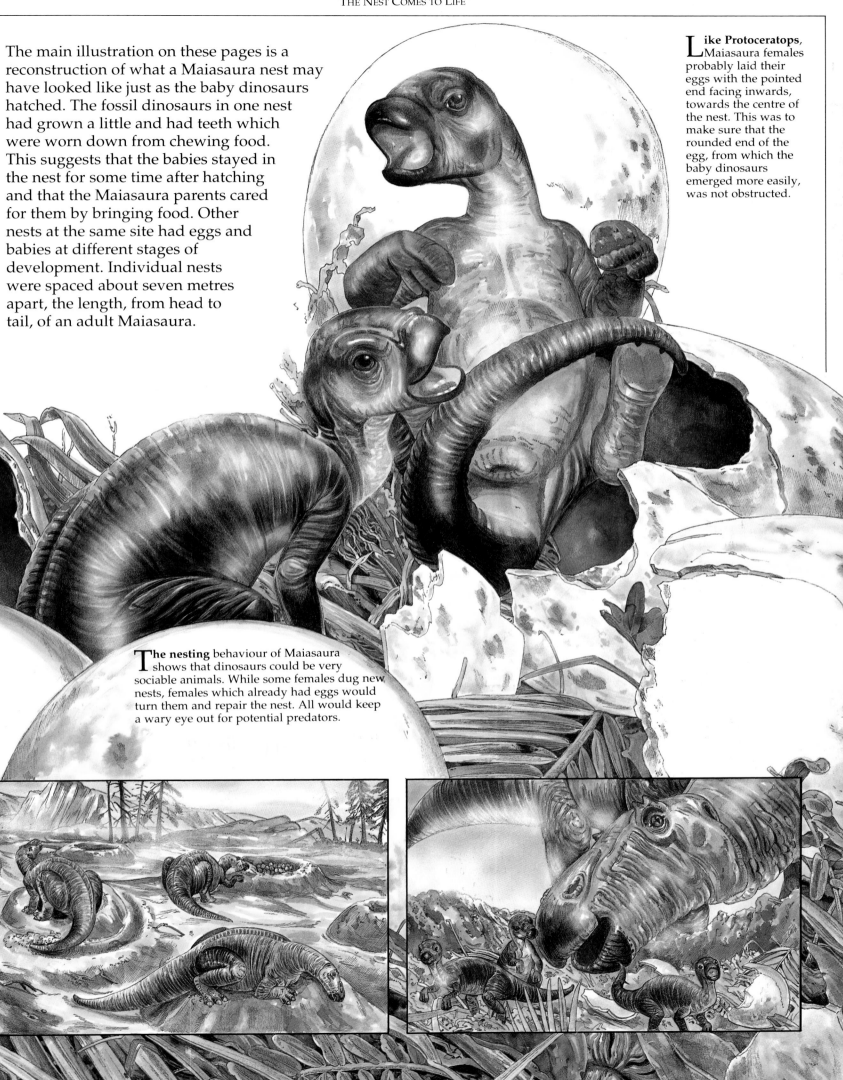

The main illustration on these pages is a reconstruction of what a Maiasaura nest may have looked like just as the baby dinosaurs hatched. The fossil dinosaurs in one nest had grown a little and had teeth which were worn down from chewing food. This suggests that the babies stayed in the nest for some time after hatching and that the Maiasaura parents cared for them by bringing food. Other nests at the same site had eggs and babies at different stages of development. Individual nests were spaced about seven metres apart, the length, from head to tail, of an adult Maiasaura.

Like Protoceratops, Maiasaura females probably laid their eggs with the pointed end facing inwards, towards the centre of the nest. This was to make sure that the rounded end of the egg, from which the baby dinosaurs emerged more easily, was not obstructed.

The nesting behaviour of Maiasaura shows that dinosaurs could be very sociable animals. While some females dug new nests, females which already had eggs would turn them and repair the nest. All would keep a wary eye out for potential predators.

Deinonychus had an unusual muscle in its leg which enabled it to kick viciously and inflict terrible injury with the huge claw on its second toe.

Iguanodon had a dagger-like claw which it used to attack predators when cornered. The spike could tear the predator's neck muscles with ease.

Tyrannosaurus' method of attack was fast and fatal. Its skull was very strong so that it could run into its prey with its jaws open without sustaining injury.

Triceratops was a herbivore but could be aggressive and would charge when threatened. An adult was more than a match for a Tyrannosaurus.

Struthiomimus had large, powerful back legs which allowed it to chase insects at high speed. Once caught in its long jaws an insect had little chance of escape.

Some dinosaurs attacked members of their own group. Pachycephalosaurus engaged in head-butting contests to decide which male was dominant.

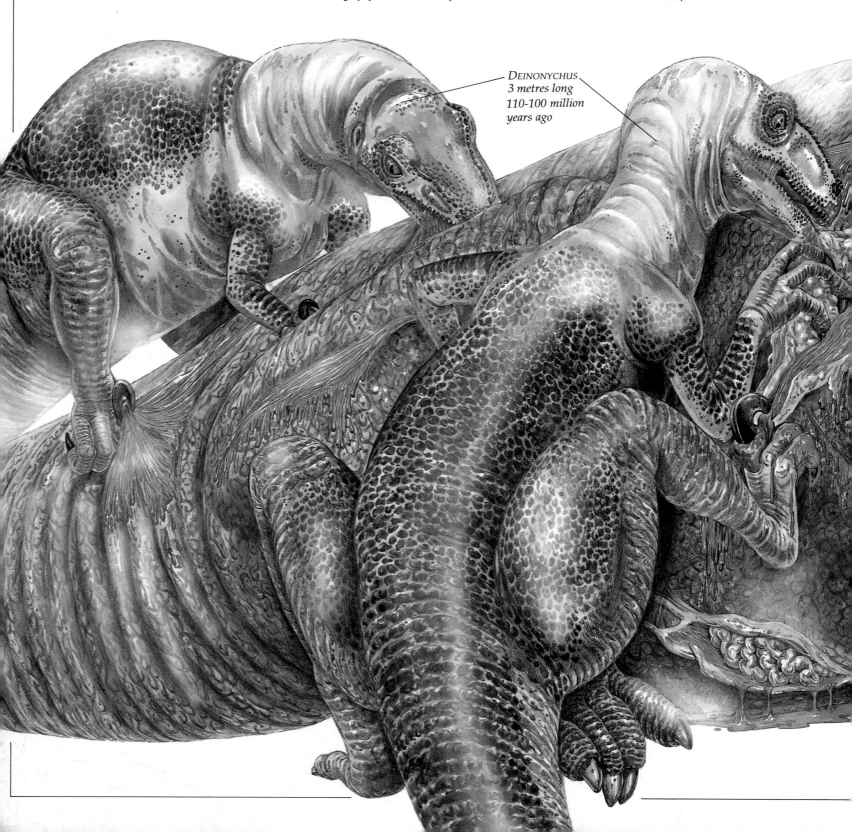

DEINONYCHUS
3 metres long
110-100 million
years ago

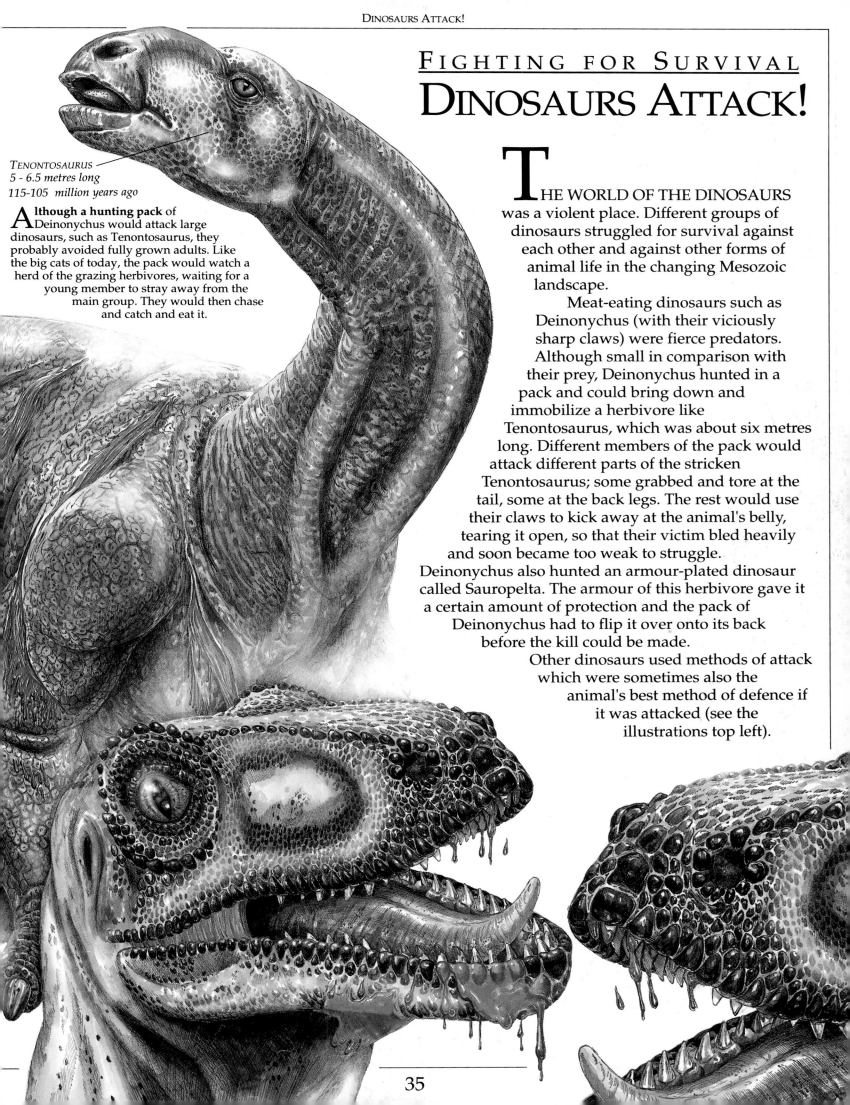

TENONTOSAURUS
5 - 6.5 metres long
115-105 million years ago

Although a hunting pack of Deinonychus would attack large dinosaurs, such as Tenontosaurus, they probably avoided fully grown adults. Like the big cats of today, the pack would watch a herd of the grazing herbivores, waiting for a young member to stray away from the main group. They would then chase and catch and eat it.

FIGHTING FOR SURVIVAL
DINOSAURS ATTACK!

THE WORLD OF THE DINOSAURS was a violent place. Different groups of dinosaurs struggled for survival against each other and against other forms of animal life in the changing Mesozoic landscape.

Meat-eating dinosaurs such as Deinonychus (with their viciously sharp claws) were fierce predators. Although small in comparison with their prey, Deinonychus hunted in a pack and could bring down and immobilize a herbivore like Tenontosaurus, which was about six metres long. Different members of the pack would attack different parts of the stricken Tenontosaurus; some grabbed and tore at the tail, some at the back legs. The rest would use their claws to kick away at the animal's belly, tearing it open, so that their victim bled heavily and soon became too weak to struggle. Deinonychus also hunted an armour-plated dinosaur called Sauropelta. The armour of this herbivore gave it a certain amount of protection and the pack of Deinonychus had to flip it over onto its back before the kill could be made.

Other dinosaurs used methods of attack which were sometimes also the animal's best method of defence if it was attacked (see the illustrations top left).

FIGHTING FOR SURVIVAL
DINOSAURS ON THE DEFENSIVE

The large round club at the end of Euoplocephalus' tail was an excellent weapon against predators. A sharp blow might not kill, but could inflict serious injury.

WHETHER PROTECTING THEMSELVES FROM ATTACK by fierce predators or fighting for their territory, dinosaurs devised many different types of defence. The thick bony plates embedded in the leathery skin of Euoplocephalus helped it withstand attacks by Albertosaurus. The pointed spines on its head and along its back could wound a predator. A persistent Albertosaurus, continuing to attack despite all the armour, would have received a heavy blow from the tail club of Euoplocephalus, perhaps laming it or even knocking it to the ground.

Leathery skin

EUOPLOCEPHALUS
6 metres long
75-64 million years ago

DINOSAUR DEFENCES

Hylaeosaurus, a heavily armour-plated dinosaur, avoided being injured in an attack by lying as flat as it could on the ground and exposing only its tough body armour and sharp spikes.

A group of Chasmosaurus defended their young by forming a defensive cluster when they were under attack. This prevented a predator from reaching the vulnerable babies.

Kentrosaurus was one of the smaller dinosaurs but it could be aggressive when attacked. By reversing into a predator, using its sharp spines as weapons, it could cause severe injuries.

Groups of herbivorous dinosaurs, such as Plateosaurus, moved around in family groups within herds, protecting weaker members by keeping them in the centre.

Some smaller dinosaurs, such as Lesothosaurus, had one of the simplest defence strategies: they ran away as fast as they could. Larger carnivores could not match their speed.

Parasaurolophus is thought to have been a good swimmer and could have escaped from a large predator, such as Tyrannosaurus, by plunging into a nearby river or lake.

Euoplocephalus' tail club was an amazing structure. It was formed from the bony plates at the end of the tail which were part of the skin armour and which had evolved to become huge and heavy. These bones had fused with each other and with the last internal bones at the end of the tail. A six-metre-long adult Euoplocephalus had a tail club that was 40 centimetres long, 60 centimetres wide and weighed several kilograms. The rest of the tail was not so heavily armoured, enabling Euoplocephalus to swing the club easily to cause the maximum amount of damage that it could to a predator such as Albertosaurus.

Tail club

A **single blow** from Euoplocephalus' tail club, aimed at Albertosaurus' ankles, could have been fatal to this fierce predator. If the blow knocked it over it is probable that the fall would have broken the animal's legs or pelvis and it would have lain helpless and dying until it was killed and eaten by other carnivores.

ALBERTOSAURUS
9 metres long
75-64 million years ago

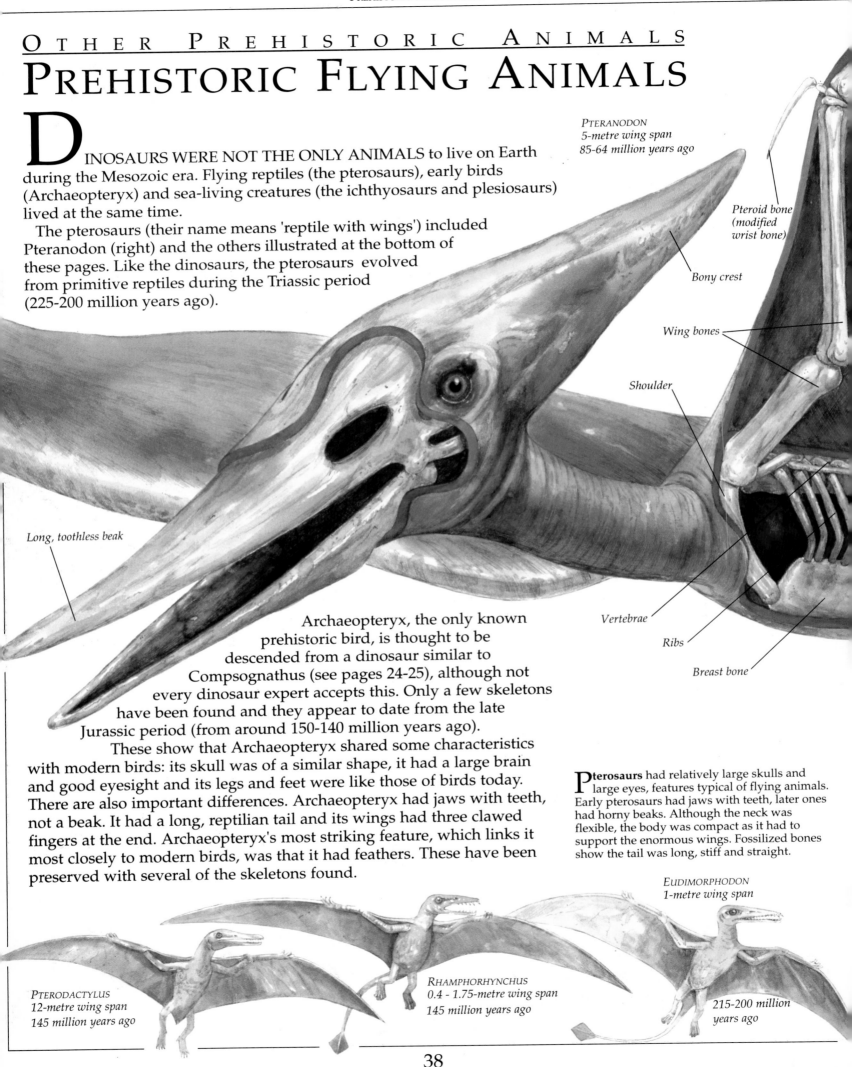

OTHER PREHISTORIC ANIMALS
PREHISTORIC FLYING ANIMALS

DINOSAURS WERE NOT THE ONLY ANIMALS to live on Earth during the Mesozoic era. Flying reptiles (the pterosaurs), early birds (Archaeopteryx) and sea-living creatures (the ichthyosaurs and plesiosaurs) lived at the same time.

The pterosaurs (their name means 'reptile with wings') included Pteranodon (right) and the others illustrated at the bottom of these pages. Like the dinosaurs, the pterosaurs evolved from primitive reptiles during the Triassic period (225-200 million years ago).

PTERANODON
5-metre wing span
85-64 million years ago

Pteroid bone (modified wrist bone)

Bony crest

Wing bones

Shoulder

Long, toothless beak

Vertebrae

Ribs

Breast bone

Archaeopteryx, the only known prehistoric bird, is thought to be descended from a dinosaur similar to Compsognathus (see pages 24-25), although not every dinosaur expert accepts this. Only a few skeletons have been found and they appear to date from the late Jurassic period (from around 150-140 million years ago).

These show that Archaeopteryx shared some characteristics with modern birds: its skull was of a similar shape, it had a large brain and good eyesight and its legs and feet were like those of birds today. There are also important differences. Archaeopteryx had jaws with teeth, not a beak. It had a long, reptilian tail and its wings had three clawed fingers at the end. Archaeopteryx's most striking feature, which links it most closely to modern birds, was that it had feathers. These have been preserved with several of the skeletons found.

Pterosaurs had relatively large skulls and large eyes, features typical of flying animals. Early pterosaurs had jaws with teeth, later ones had horny beaks. Although the neck was flexible, the body was compact as it had to support the enormous wings. Fossilized bones show the tail was long, stiff and straight.

EUDIMORPHODON
1-metre wing span

PTERODACTYLUS
12-metre wing span
145 million years ago

RHAMPHORHYNCHUS
0.4 - 1.75-metre wing span
145 million years ago

215-200 million years ago

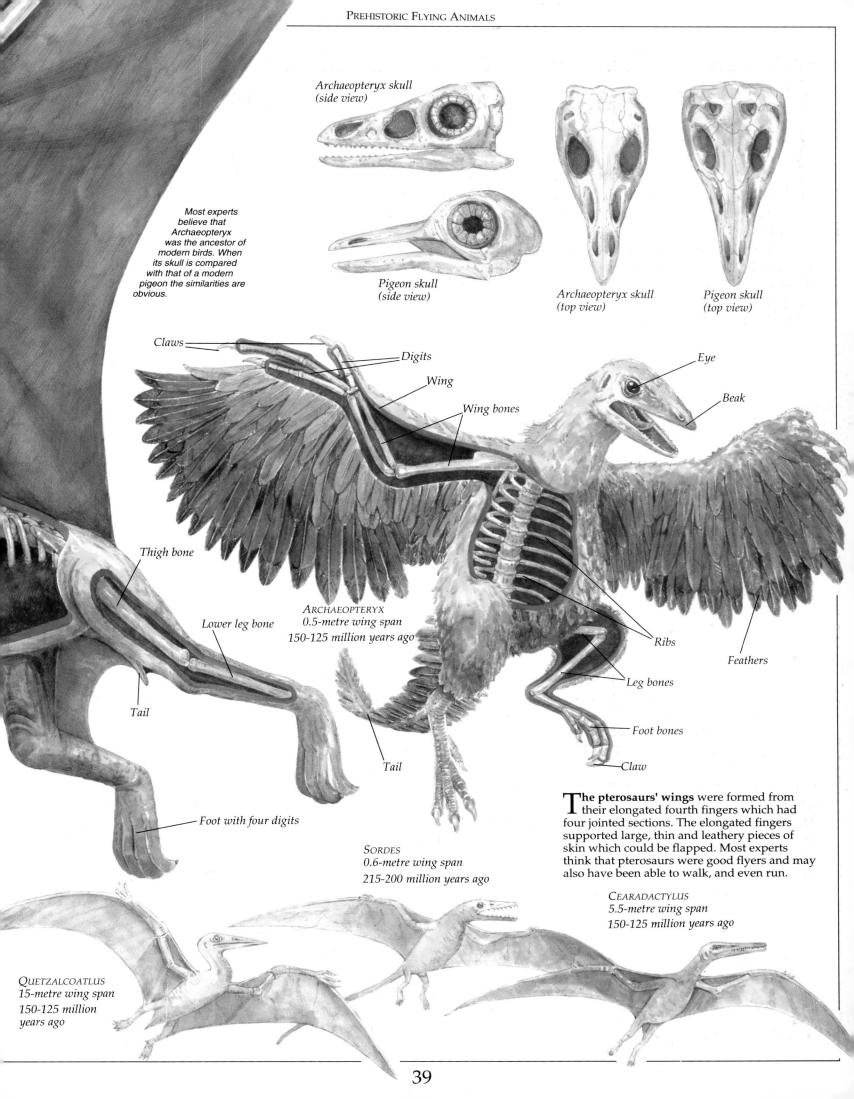

Archaeopteryx skull
(side view)

Pigeon skull
(side view)

Archaeopteryx skull
(top view)

Pigeon skull
(top view)

Most experts
believe that
Archaeopteryx
was the ancestor of
modern birds. When
its skull is compared
with that of a modern
pigeon the similarities are
obvious.

Claws

Digits

Wing

Wing bones

Eye

Beak

Thigh bone

Lower leg bone

ARCHAEOPTERYX
0.5-metre wing span
150-125 million years ago

Ribs

Feathers

Tail

Leg bones

Foot with four digits

Foot bones

Claw

Tail

SORDES
0.6-metre wing span
215-200 million years ago

The pterosaurs' wings were formed from their elongated fourth fingers which had four jointed sections. The elongated fingers supported large, thin and leathery pieces of skin which could be flapped. Most experts think that pterosaurs were good flyers and may also have been able to walk, and even run.

CEARADACTYLUS
5.5-metre wing span
150-125 million years ago

QUETZALCOATLUS
15-metre wing span
150-125 million
years ago

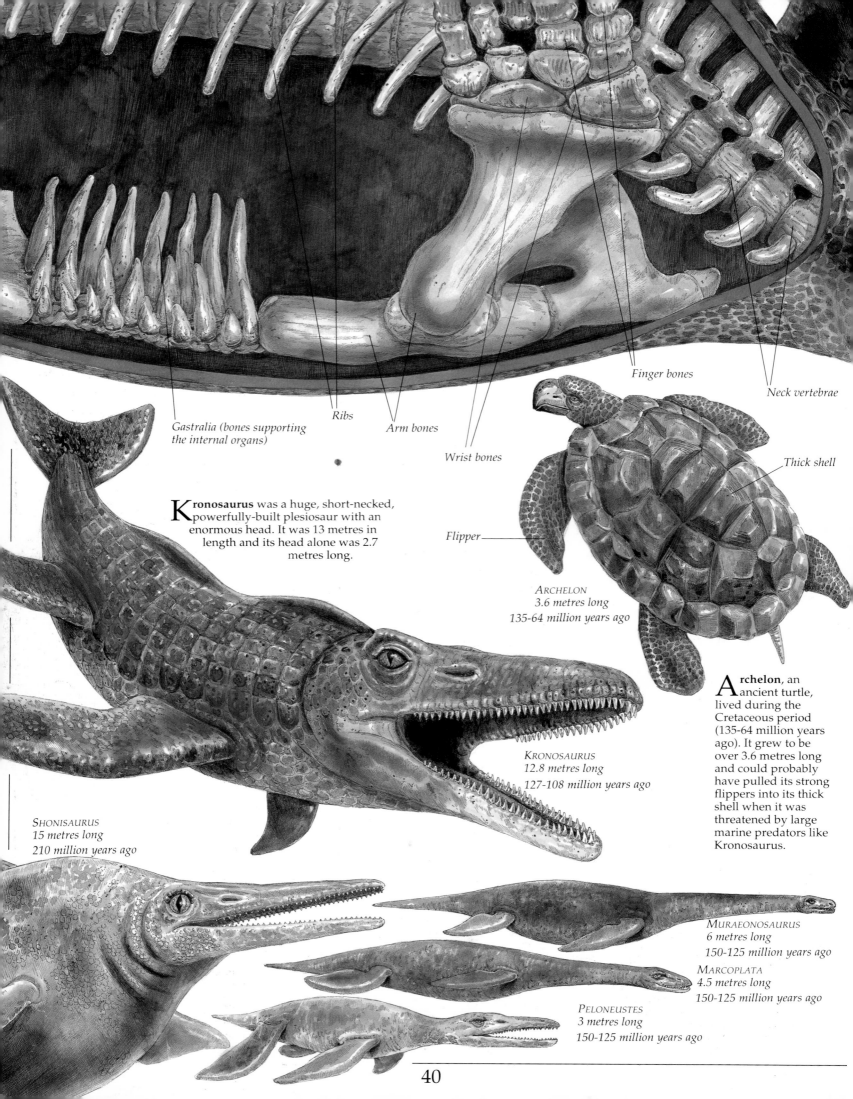

Gastralia (bones supporting
the internal organs)

Ribs

Arm bones

Wrist bones

Finger bones

Neck vertebrae

Thick shell

Flipper

Kronosaurus was a huge, short-necked,
powerfully-built plesiosaur with an
enormous head. It was 13 metres in
length and its head alone was 2.7
metres long.

ARCHELON
3.6 metres long
135-64 million years ago

KRONOSAURUS
12.8 metres long
127-108 million years ago

Archelon, an
ancient turtle,
lived during the
Cretaceous period
(135-64 million years
ago). It grew to be
over 3.6 metres long
and could probably
have pulled its strong
flippers into its thick
shell when it was
threatened by large
marine predators like
Kronosaurus.

SHONISAURUS
15 metres long
210 million years ago

MURAEONOSAURUS
6 metres long
150-125 million years ago

MARCOPLATA
4.5 metres long
150-125 million years ago

PELONEUSTES
3 metres long
150-125 million years ago

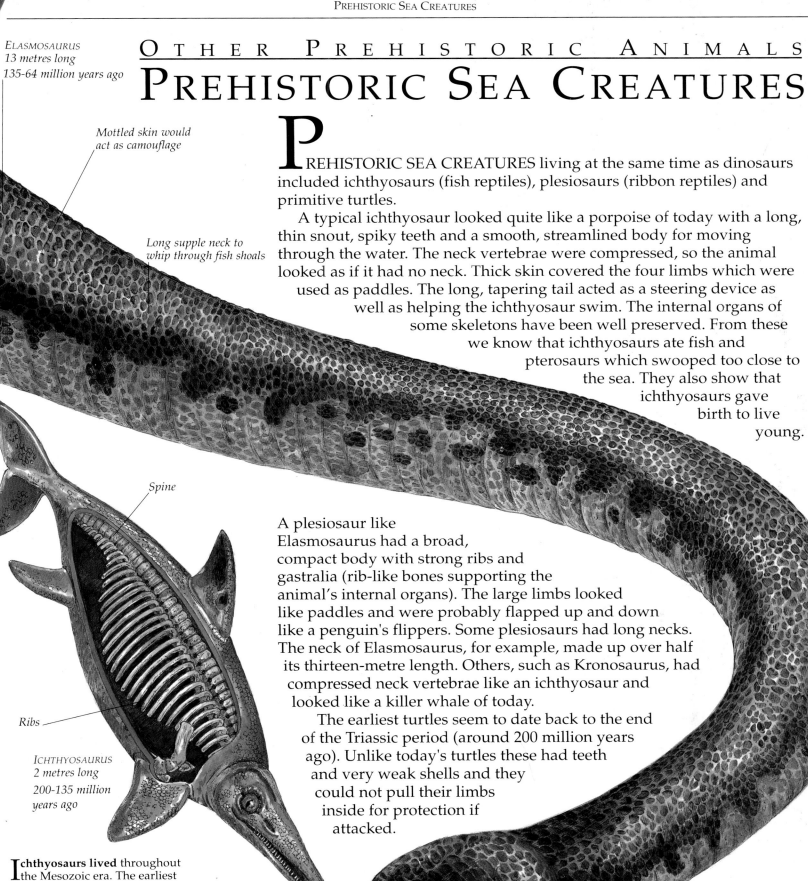

PREHISTORIC SEA CREATURES

ELASMOSAURUS
13 metres long
135-64 million years ago

Mottled skin would
act as camouflage

Long supple neck to
whip through fish shoals

P REHISTORIC SEA CREATURES living at the same time as dinosaurs included ichthyosaurs (fish reptiles), plesiosaurs (ribbon reptiles) and primitive turtles.

A typical ichthyosaur looked quite like a porpoise of today with a long, thin snout, spiky teeth and a smooth, streamlined body for moving through the water. The neck vertebrae were compressed, so the animal looked as if it had no neck. Thick skin covered the four limbs which were used as paddles. The long, tapering tail acted as a steering device as well as helping the ichthyosaur swim. The internal organs of some skeletons have been well preserved. From these we know that ichthyosaurs ate fish and pterosaurs which swooped too close to the sea. They also show that ichthyosaurs gave birth to live young.

Spine

A plesiosaur like Elasmosaurus had a broad, compact body with strong ribs and gastralia (rib-like bones supporting the animal's internal organs). The large limbs looked like paddles and were probably flapped up and down like a penguin's flippers. Some plesiosaurs had long necks. The neck of Elasmosaurus, for example, made up over half its thirteen-metre length. Others, such as Kronosaurus, had compressed neck vertebrae like an ichthyosaur and looked like a killer whale of today.

The earliest turtles seem to date back to the end of the Triassic period (around 200 million years ago). Unlike today's turtles these had teeth and very weak shells and they could not pull their limbs inside for protection if attacked.

Ribs

ICHTHYOSAURUS
2 metres long
200-135 million
years ago

I **chthyosaurs lived** throughout the Mesozoic era. The earliest fossils have been found in rocks from the late Triassic period (about 200 million years ago). However, other fossils show that ichthyosaurs were at their most abundant in the Jurassic period (200-135 million years ago) and a few were still around in the Cretaceous period (135-64 million years ago). All were well adapted to living in water, although no-one can explain their ancestry. No fossils of sea-living archosaurs from which they could have evolved have ever been found.

E **lasmosaurus** could swim very fast. The muscles of its flipper-like limbs were large and powerful and were joined to a strong skeleton. It probably caught small fish by whipping its head from side to side and scooping several into its long mouth at once. Its sharp, pointed teeth could interlock, preventing the fish from escaping before it could swallow them.

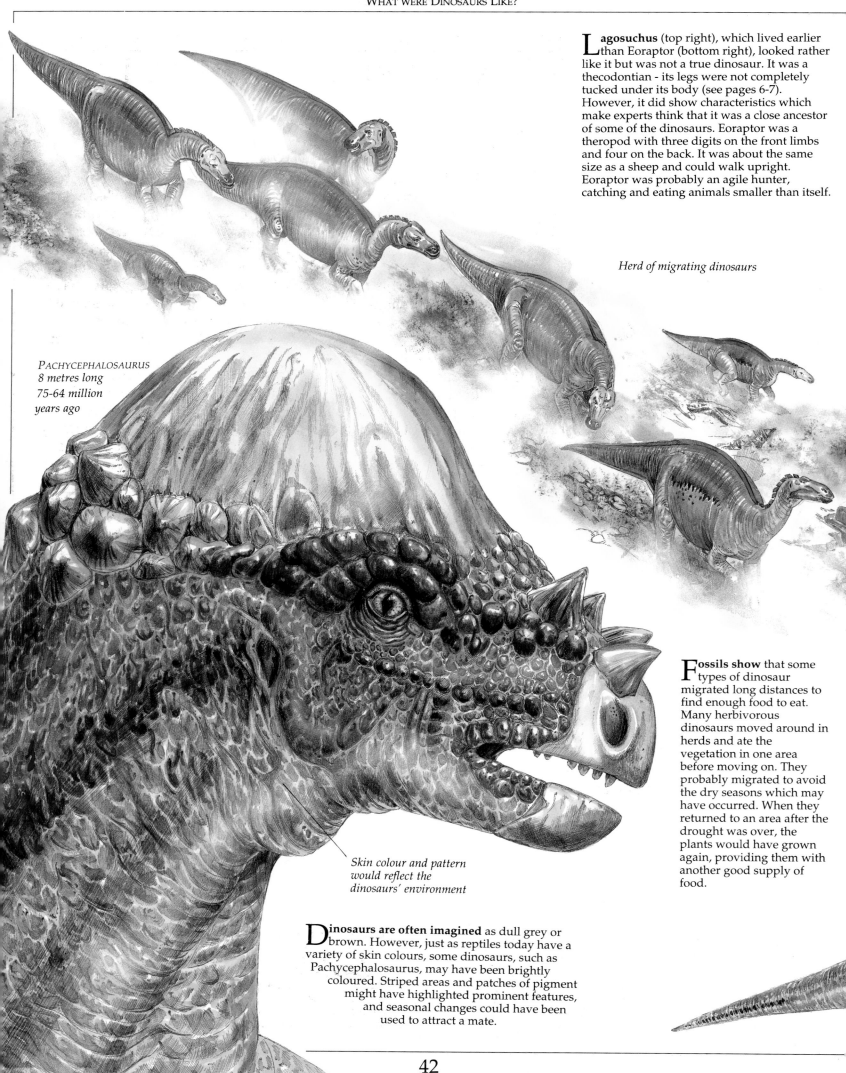

Lagosuchus (top right), which lived earlier than Eoraptor (bottom right), looked rather like it but was not a true dinosaur. It was a thecodontian - its legs were not completely tucked under its body (see pages 6-7). However, it did show characteristics which make experts think that it was a close ancestor of some of the dinosaurs. Eoraptor was a theropod with three digits on the front limbs and four on the back. It was about the same size as a sheep and could walk upright. Eoraptor was probably an agile hunter, catching and eating animals smaller than itself.

Herd of migrating dinosaurs

*PACHYCEPHALOSAURUS
8 metres long
75-64 million
years ago*

*Skin colour and pattern
would reflect the
dinosaurs' environment*

Fossils show that some types of dinosaur migrated long distances to find enough food to eat. Many herbivorous dinosaurs moved around in herds and ate the vegetation in one area before moving on. They probably migrated to avoid the dry seasons which may have occurred. When they returned to an area after the drought was over, the plants would have grown again, providing them with another good supply of food.

Dinosaurs are often imagined as dull grey or brown. However, just as reptiles today have a variety of skin colours, some dinosaurs, such as Pachycephalosaurus, may have been brightly coloured. Striped areas and patches of pigment might have highlighted prominent features, and seasonal changes could have been used to attract a mate.

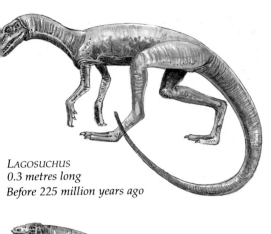

LAGOSUCHUS
0.3 metres long
Before 225 million years ago

EORAPTOR
1 metre long
225 million years ago

MYSTERIES AND MYTHS
WHAT WERE DINOSAURS LIKE?

WE HAVE LEARNT A GREAT DEAL ABOUT DINOSAURS from their fossilized remains but many things about them are still a mystery. For example, we do not know much about how dinosaurs evolved from their primitive reptile ancestors, how they were related to each other or how they developed during the 161 million years they lived on Earth.

Remains of the earliest known dinosaur were found in rocks in the Andes in Argentina in 1991. Eoraptor, as it was called, is thought to have lived 225 million years ago. It was only one metre long, the same size as a large dog today. Because Eoraptor was so different from primitive reptiles, experts think that dinosaurs had already been evolving for about ten million years by the time that it appeared.

It is also difficult to know exactly how dinosaurs lived or precisely what they looked like. Detailed studies of dinosaur skeletons show the shapes of the different groups of dinosaurs and the features by which they recognized each other. However, because soft tissues, such as skin, hearts and intestines, are rarely preserved with bones, it is impossible to tell how their bodies worked or the colours and textures of their skins. One unanswered question is: were dinosaurs cold-blooded, like the reptiles of today, or were they warm-blooded, like mammals?

The behaviour of the dinosaurs is another tantalizing mystery. Fossils may give clues about breeding habits, diet, whether dinosaurs migrated and whether they lived in herds or were solitary. In most cases we can only guess what life for dinosaurs was really like.

Two models of Iguanodon

Reconstructing a dinosaur skeleton can be difficult as the bones are often scattered and not all of them may be there anyway. Today's reconstruction of Iguanodon (far left) looks very different from the model made for the Great Exhibition in 1854 (near left). Notice the wrong shape given to the body and the tail, and the thumb spike, which was placed on the nose!

As the sky darkened after the impact of the meteor, the dust would initially have caused dramatic and colourful sunsets. These would have lasted only a few days and then the world of the dinosaurs and other animals of the late Cretaceous period would have been plunged into darkness.

The darkness would have persisted for many months, cutting out the sunlight vital to plant growth. The choking clouds may have contained toxic gases. Plants on the ground would have started to die immediately. The only ones which could survive would have been those that had produced seeds.

The shortage of plants would have meant the herbivores of the time starved. Large ones, mainly the dinosaurs, would have died quickly because they needed to eat so much to survive. Smaller ones, which needed much less food, may have managed to live by eating seeds and berries.

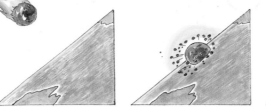

The meteor which is believed to have hit the Earth 64 million years ago would have caused an enormous explosion as it began to vaporize in the Earth's atmosphere and then collided with the planet's surface (see diagrams right). The impact would have changed the meteor from a solid object with a diameter of about 15 kilometres into a huge cloud of dust and water vapour. This would have spread out into the atmosphere, shrouding the Earth in darkness.

MYSTERIES AND MYTHS
WHY DID DINOSAURS DISAPPEAR?

W E MAY NEVER KNOW FOR CERTAIN just what caused the extinction of dinosaurs and other prehistoric life forms at the end of the Cretaceous period, 64 million years ago. Many scientists believe that a huge meteor hit the Earth, causing a massive cloud of debris to cover the planet for several months, cutting out sunlight and causing dramatic changes in climate. Large animals, such as the dinosaurs, died while some small mammals, lizards and snakes managed to survive.

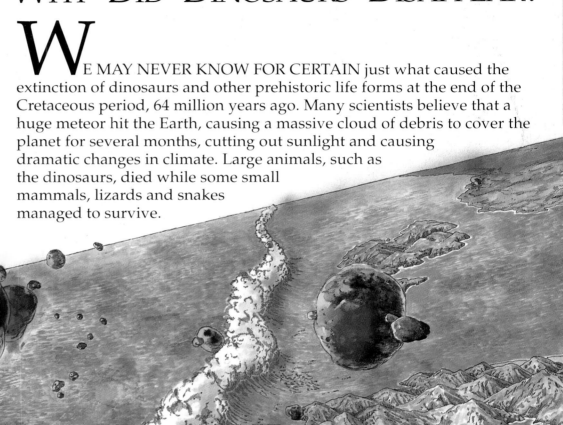

Carcasses of the dead herbivores could have fed carnivorous animals, including the large carnivorous dinosaurs, for a short time but, as they were eaten, or decayed where they had died, this food would have disappeared and dinosaurs, such as Tyrannosaurus, would also have perished.

As the cloud began to lift, the weak sunlight would have revealed a bleak and barren landscape with no plants and few signs of life. Small animals, such as the tiny mammals, would have survived by scavenging and eating insects, such as dragonflies and beetles, which had lived through the crisis.

It probably took millions of years of evolution during the Palaeocene and Eocene periods (64 to 38 million years ago) to produce the incredible variety of mammals, birds, insects, reptiles and amphibians which could be found by the end of the Oligocene period, around 25 million years ago.

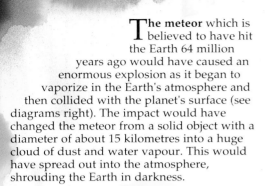

GLOSSARY

Amnion The protective membrane which surrounds an embryo as it develops inside an egg or inside its mother's body.

Amphibian An animal which is able to live both in water and on land, such as frogs and toads.

Ancestor An animal from which another animal is descended.

Archosaurs A major group of reptiles from which the dinosaurs, pterosaurs and modern crocodiles evolved.

Biped An animal which normally walks on only two feet. Many of the dinosaurs were bipeds.

Carnivore An animal which eats meat as the major part of its diet. A carnivore can be a predator or a scavenger, or a mixture of both.

Cold-blooded animals Animals which have no way of maintaining a constant body temperature. Their body temperature changes as the temperature of their surroundings goes up and down. They rely on heat from the sun's rays to provide them with enough warmth to be active during the day. Examples include reptiles and insects. Most experts think that dinosaurs were cold-blooded.

Conifers Trees, such as firs, pines and yews, which produce cones to carry their reproductive spores.

Cretaceous period The third period of the Mesozoic era which lasted from 135 million years ago until 64 million years ago. The dinosaurs, pterosaurs, plesiosaurs and other groups of animals became extinct at the end of the Cretaceous period.

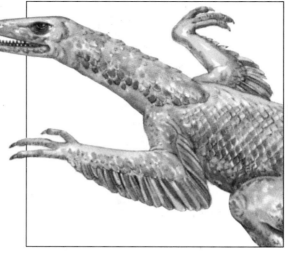

Cycads Short, palm-tree-like plants common during the Mesozoic era.

Digit A finger or toe.

Dinosaur A land-living reptile which lived between 225 and 64 million years ago. 'Dinosaur' comes from a Greek word meaning 'terrible reptile'. The dinosaurs evolved into two groups, ornithischian dinosaurs and saurischian dinosaurs, according to the arrangement of the ischium and pubis bones within their pelvis.

Dominant A dominant animal or group of animals is the most important and/or the most abundant in an environment. Dinosaurs were dominant during the Mesozoic era.

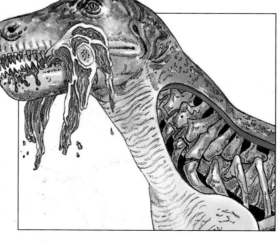

Evolution A process by which a population of animals or plants gradually changes over many generations.

Evolve To change in form or appearance over many generations.

Extinction When all members of a group of plants or animals are dead. The dinosaurs and many other prehistoric creatures became extinct 64 million years ago.

Ferns Low-growing plants with fronds (leaf-like structures which carry the reproductive part of the plant).

Flowering plants Plants which have leaves and modified leaves (flowers) carrying the reproductive parts of the plant.

Fossil The preserved remains of something which once lived. Fossils are usually formed when a dead animal or plant is buried and then compressed by the weight of whatever buried it.

Gastralia Rib-like bones found in the abdomen of some animals to support the internal organs.

Gastroliths Stones found in the stomachs of some dinosaurs which helped to break up tough plant food so that it could be digested more easily.

Hatchling Young animal which has recently hatched from an egg.

Herbivore An animal which eats plant material.

Ichthyosaurs Sea-living reptiles which lived between 225 and 64 million years ago and which had streamlined fish-shaped bodies.

Invertebrates Animals without backbones (for example, insects).

Ischium One of the bones of the pelvis (the other is the pubis).

Jurassic period The second period of the Mesozoic era which lasted from 200 million years ago until 135 million years ago.

Ligaments Tough sheets or threads which link bone to bone at joints.

Mammals A group of warm-blooded animals which produce milk to feed their young and which have hair or fur.

Mesozoic era The period of time between 225 and 64 million years ago which incorporates the Triassic, Jurassic and Cretaceous periods.

Muscles Structures which produce movement in an animal's body.

Oesophagus The tube which extends from the throat into the stomach.

Ornithischian dinosaur A member of one of the two groups of dinosaur (the other group is the saurischian group). In ornithischian dinosaurs the two bones of the pelvis (the ischium and pubis) pointed in the same direction, as in birds. Ornithischian dinosaurs were all herbivores.

Pelvis The part of the skeleton commonly known as the hip.

Predator An animal which hunts another animal for food.

Prehistoric creature An animal which lived before the time that humans evolved.

Pterosaurs Flying reptiles which lived between 225 and 64 million years ago and which were distant relatives of the dinosaurs.

Pubis One of the bones of the pelvis (the other is the ischium).

Reptiles A group of cold-blooded animals which includes the snakes, lizards, crocodiles, turtles, tortoises, and the now-extinct dinosaurs, pterosaurs, ichthyosaurs and plesiosaurs.

Saurischian dinosaur A member of one of the two groups of dinosaur (the other group is the ornithischian group). In saurischian dinosaurs and other reptiles, the two bones of the pelvis (the ischium and pubis) point in different directions. Some saurischian dinosaurs, such as Plateosaurus, were herbivores and some, such as Tyrannosaurus, were carnivores.

Scavenger An animal which feeds on the carcass of an animal which has been killed by another animal or has died because of disease or injury.

Tendons The sheets or threads which join muscles to bones at joints.

Territory An area of land where an animal, or group of animals, lives. A territory is often defended fiercely.

Thecodontians The group of archosaurs from which dinosaurs, pterosaurs and crocodiles evolved during the Triassic period.

Theropod A group of carnivorous dinosaurs which were bipeds.

Toxic Poisonous.

Trachea The tube which extends from the throat into the lungs.

Triassic period The first period of the Mesozoic era which lasted from 225 million years ago until 200 million years ago. The dinosaurs first appeared during the Triassic period.

Vascular land plants Plants which have tube-like structures to carry water from their roots to their leaves. This development allowed plants to grow on the land, rather than submerged in water.

Vertebrae The bones which form the backbone of an animal.

Warm-blooded animals Animals which can maintain the same body temperature, even when the temperature of their surroundings goes up and down. In cold conditions this is an advantage because, unlike cold-blooded animals, they can still be active and hunt for food. Mammals and birds are all warm-blooded.

INDEX